SO VEGAN

EASY

ROXY POPE + BEN POOK

SO VEGAN

EASY

ROXY POPE + BEN POOK

PHOTOGRAPHY
YUKI SUGIURA

MICHAEL  JOSEPH

WELCOME TO SO VEGAN

15 MINS OR LESS

15–30 MINS

30 MINS OR MORE

WELCOME TO SO VEGAN

We're Roxy and Ben – aka SO VEGAN. We're a plant-powered couple who simply believe that the food we choose to eat can have a positive impact on our health and the planet. But not just any old food. We're talking about vegan dishes that deliver lots of flavour with minimal fuss.

Like so many others, food is almost always on our minds. We wake up every morning thinking about what wonderful food we're going to fill our bellies with that day. Spending most of our waking hours in the kitchen probably helps, but more than anything we're convinced that cooking is a hobby that can and should be fun. It's something we humans spend our lives doing more than almost anything else, so there's no reason why we shouldn't try to enjoy it as much as possible.

But all too often, cooking nutritious vegan food is made to seem complicated and time-consuming, which makes it difficult to enjoy. That's why in this book – *EASY* – you'll find 100 super simple lunches, dinners and desserts that will fundamentally make your life easier. We're talking about straightforward and speedy meals that are not only good for you and the planet but are also a total joy to cook.

With that in mind, we decided to split this book into four chapters: 15 Mins or Less, 15–30 Mins, 30 Mins or More and Desserts.

We want you to pick up *EASY* and quickly find meals that will seamlessly fit into your busy lives. This way you can easily plan your recipes knowing how long they will take to cook. Need a super-speedy midweek dinner? Go straight to 15 Mins or Less. Need something to impress friends or family on a Sunday afternoon? Take a peek at 30 Mins or More. Aside from the desserts, every recipe is a delicious meal that will work as a dinner or a lunch, and quite often both.

Our cooking philosophy follows a number of simple principles: we want to inspire people to cook vegan food that is accessible, nutritious and flavoursome. These guiding principles work as a framework that informs all our recipes, so expect to find lots of mouth-watering meals that are affordable, use easy-to-find ingredients and are often high in protein or can easily be made gluten-free.

We also created this book because it has never been more important to eat more plants. Study after study has shown that reducing the amount of meat and dairy we eat – and choosing plant-based foods instead – can go a huge way towards helping us combat the climate crisis. Our platform – SO VEGAN – exists because we want to give you the tools to take on this challenge, and *EASY* is the next step in this mission.

So let this book be your toolbox full of fuss-free recipes that will help you eat more wholesome, planet-friendly food while enjoying one of life's greatest pleasures: cooking.

A LOT HAS HAPPENED OVER THE PAST FEW YEARS

On a personal level, we started a family! SO VEGAN now has two mini-members who go by the names of Maya and Esi. You'll see them pop up a few times throughout the book (and steal the show like they always do).

We also moved into a new kitchen studio in Peckham, south-east London, where we developed all the recipes for this book, and we launched our very own SO VEGAN recipe app, which has been really well received by our amazing community.

From a broader perspective, a lot has also changed in the world around us. Society is still working out how best to recover from the pandemic, and we're in the midst of a cost-of-living crisis that is putting the livelihoods of so many people at risk.

There's a lot of uncertainty right now, but what's often so great about cookbooks is that not only do they capture a moment in time, they also provide useful ways to overcome some of the hurdles in front of us – and we really believe *EASY* is no different.

When we started SO VEGAN way back in 2016, we didn't really have any preconceived ideas about the type of food we wanted to make – we just wanted to create delicious vegan meals. Instinctively, however, we also developed recipes that were easy. Why? Because that's just how we've always loved to cook. You've probably gathered by now that we're obsessed with food, but that doesn't mean we want to spend longer than is necessary in the kitchen – especially after a long day at work.

Fast-forward to today and our attitude hasn't changed. In fact, we're now driven by a mission to create a healthier and happier world – and as far as we're concerned, that involves making delicious and nutritious vegan food accessible to anyone.

So within these pages you'll discover recipes that are not only practical and affordable but that also give your body lots of the nutrients it needs to help you feel good. These are simple meals that feature ingredients you'll be able to find in your local supermarket, not obscure and expensive stores.

Accessibility is everything to us. It's about lowering barriers and encouraging a mass movement of people to reduce the amount of meat and dairy they eat – switching to more vegan food instead. This is by far one of the most effective ways we can have a positive impact on the planet.

You'll also find some recipes that cater for families with small mouths to feed – and we make an effort to point these out in the descriptions underneath the recipe titles. While it's not always practical, we try to eat together as a family as often as we can, and a few of our family favourites have made their way into this book, including our Tomato + Fennel Macaroni Soup (page 165) and Sweet Potato + Chickpea Turmeric Curry (page 103).

Hopefully you'll also flick through these pages and sense how much fun we had creating this book. For various reasons, we've spent the past couple of years reflecting on the things that matter the most to us. What we're constantly reminded of is the momentous role food plays in our shared experiences – and that's exactly why it gives us so much enjoyment.

Food culture – whether it's sitting around a dinner table at home, ordering your favourite takeaway or travelling around the world to try new cuisines – brings people together in a way that feels more precious now than it has in a long time.

At every opportunity – from the recipes and photography to the design of these pages – we tried as hard as we could to channel this sense of joy and fulfilment into *EASY*, because our hope is that it will serve you – the reader – with those similar shared experiences that really do matter the most.

So when we describe this book to people, we often say it's a celebration of vegan food. To be more precise, we guess you could say it's a celebration of *our version* of vegan food, which is wonderfully nutritious, devilishly delicious and – you guessed it – super easy.

We hope you enjoy celebrating vegan food with us.

Big love,

ROXY + BEN, SO VEGAN

THINGS TO LOOK OUT FOR

Throughout the book you might notice the tags at the bottom of the page, which we use to identify recipes that are a good source of protein, gluten-free, freezer-friendly or cook in one pot/tray/pan. These are designed to help you quickly flick through the chapters to find meals that suit your requirements.

Our recipes use lots of whole foods, which means either they're already gluten-free or they can be easily made gluten-free with one or two small adjustments – and we'll explain how when necessary. Likewise, components of a dish may or may not be freezer-friendly, so where necessary we explain what you can or can't freeze.

Meals tagged as 'one' involve using a single pot, tray or pan to cook the recipe. These recipes might also use a couple of bowls or a blender in the preparation, but importantly the cooking is all done in only one dish.

If you want to know the nutritional information for each recipe – such as the protein, salt and calories in each portion – head to the back of the book, where you'll find a table breaking all of this down for you.

We've been vegan for over eight years, which means we're well and truly converted to the ways of the tofu. You'll spot this underrated ingredient popping up in noodles, curries and even on toast. We almost always use extra firm tofu, which doesn't require pressing, thus reducing the amount of preparation time. Most extra firm brands only require draining the block of tofu, but if your tofu is on the soft and soggy side, you'll need to press it under a heavy object for 10–20 minutes, or until most of the water has drained out.

Vegan yoghurts and creams have come a long way in the past few years. There are now a few brands to choose from, but it's useful to know which styles are best when it comes to recreating our recipes. The general rule of thumb is that oat-based yoghurts and creams are usually less sweet than soy-based versions. As a result, we find they add a more balanced flavour to our dishes – but we include our preference (oat or soy) as a suggestion whenever these appear in our recipes.

Budget permitting, you might want to consider investing in a few good-quality ingredients that we use frequently throughout the book – and which will really help elevate these dishes. A lot has already been said about using good-quality salt and pepper and the difference they make to dishes – our preference is to use sea salt and freshly ground black pepper.

When we cook with olive oil, we'll use regular olive oil, which is refined and therefore has a higher smoking point, so it's less likely to burn. But when we add olive oil at the end of the cooking process, such as in a salad dressing or drizzled over a bowl of pasta, we love to use extra virgin olive oil. It's unrefined, which helps the oil preserve so many of the delicate flavours that can totally transform a dish.

But as with all of these suggestions, we recommend using whatever you already have in the kitchen and whatever is within your budget.

15 MINS OR LESS

TOMATO + BUTTER BEAN SUMAC SALAD

Sumac is a super versatile spice with a citrus-like flavour – and when we're not adding it to salad dressings we're using it to roast veggies or sprinkle over warm flatbreads. If you can't find beef tomatoes, regular ones will do – just be sure they're very ripe. This salad is fantastic on its own for a light meal or served as part of a big spread.

EQUIPMENT: **LARGE MIXING BOWL / BAKING TRAY**

SERVES **3–4** / PREP **5 MINS** / COOK **10 MINS**

200g crusty bread, cubed

olive oil

salt + pepper

3 dates, pitted + chopped

1 tbsp balsamic vinegar

2 tsp sumac

3 beef tomatoes (750g), thinly sliced

2 shallots, peeled + thinly sliced

1 x 400g tin of butter beans, drained + rinsed

a large handful of fresh mint (20g), leaves picked, plus extra for topping

1 Preheat the oven to 180°C fan/200°C/gas 6. Put the bread cubes into a large mixing bowl with a drizzle of olive oil and pinches of salt and pepper. Toss to combine, then transfer to a baking tray and bake for 10 minutes, or until golden brown.

2 In the same mixing bowl combine 4 tablespoons of olive oil with the dates, vinegar and 1½ teaspoons of sumac. Add the tomatoes, shallots and beans, then tear up the mint leaves and add them to the bowl along with the baked bread. Carefully toss the salad with your fingers.

3 Serve on a large plate and top with the remaining ½ teaspoon of sumac and a few more mint leaves.

GLUTEN-FREE (USE GF BREAD)

ONE-TRAY

LEMONGRASS + COCONUT CURRY

This is our go-to curry when we want something a little lighter during the warmer seasons. If you don't have a food processor or blender, you can use a pestle and mortar or simply chop the ingredients as finely as possible. Don't be shy when adding the fresh herbs, because they bring lots of aromatics to this dish.

EQUIPMENT: BLENDER OR FOOD PROCESSOR / WOK OR FRYING PAN / SAUCEPAN

SERVES 3 / PREP 10 MINS / COOK 5 MINS

5 garlic cloves, peeled

a thumb of fresh ginger
(30g), peeled

3 lemongrass stalks,
outer leaves peeled,
roughly chopped

2 green chillies

a large handful of fresh
Thai basil or regular
basil (20g), plus extra

a bunch of fresh coriander
(30g), plus extra

½ tsp ground cumin

2 x 400ml tins of
coconut milk

vegetable oil

salt + pepper

160g rice noodles

150g mangetout

1 carrot, peeled
into ribbons

1 To create the green paste, put the garlic, ginger, lemongrass, 1 green chilli (seeds removed if you don't like it hot), basil, coriander and cumin into a high-speed blender or food processor with 4 tablespoons of the coconut milk and blend until smooth.

2 Heat a drizzle of oil in a wok or frying pan on a high heat. Add the green paste and fry for 1 minute. Then tip in the rest of the coconut milk and heat for a few minutes until hot. Taste and season to your liking with generous pinches of salt and pepper.

3 Meanwhile, cook the noodles according to the packet instructions until al dente, then drain.

4 Add the mangetout and carrot ribbons to the wok and cook for 30 seconds. Then add the noodles to bowls and pour over the curry. To finish, slice the remaining green chilli and sprinkle it over the top, along with a few coriander and basil leaves.

FREEZER-FRIENDLY (WITHOUT NOODLES)

GLUTEN-FREE (USE GF NOODLES)

CREAMY AVOCADO SALAD

This glorious salad is not shy of flavour. Paprika-spiced croutons, a tangy creamy dressing and avocado all come together in a seriously satisfying meal, which we think works just as well as a lunch or a light dinner.

EQUIPMENT: **SMALL BOWL / ROASTING TRAY / BLENDER**

SERVES **4** / PREP **10 MINS** / COOK **5 MINS**

70g cashews

2 slices of crusty bread, cubed

olive oil

1 tsp paprika

salt + pepper

3 tbsp mixed seeds (we use pumpkin + sunflower)

1 little gem lettuce, leaves separated

2 avocados, peeled + quartered

½ a lemon, juice only

1 garlic clove, peeled

1 tsp Dijon mustard

1 tbsp capers, plus 1 tbsp caper juice

120ml plant-based milk (we use oat)

1 Preheat the oven to 200°C fan/220°C/gas 7. Put the cashews into a small bowl and cover with hot water straight from a kettle. Leave to soak while you carry out the next steps.

2 Place the bread cubes on one side of a large roasting tray and toss with a drizzle of olive oil, the paprika and pinches of salt and pepper. Place the seeds on the other side of the tray and roast for 5–10 minutes, or until the bread is golden.

3 Meanwhile, arrange the gem lettuce leaves and avocados on a large serving plate.

4 Drain the cashews and put them into a blender with the lemon juice, garlic, mustard, capers, caper juice and plant-based milk. Blend until smooth, then drizzle the dressing all over the leaves and avocado. Top the salad with the hot toasted seeds and bread from the oven, and finish with an extra sprinkling of salt.

GLUTEN-FREE (USE GF BREAD)
ONE-TRAY

CREAMY PESTO ROSSO GNOCCHI

'Rosso' simply translates as 'red' and it's an appropriate word to describe this vibrant dish. Inspired by the Sicilian pesto alla trapanese, our version uses sun-dried tomatoes and roasted red peppers to create a rich and comforting sauce for the gnocchi.

EQUIPMENT: **FOOD PROCESSOR OR BLENDER / FRYING PAN / SAUCEPAN**

SERVES **4** / PREP **5 MINS** / COOK **10 MINS**

40g blanched almonds

1 sprig of fresh rosemary, leaves picked

60g sun-dried tomatoes in oil, plus 3 tbsp oil from the jar

300g jarred roasted red peppers, drained

2 garlic cloves, peeled

salt + pepper

80ml vegan cream (we use oat)

600g vegan gnocchi

vegan Parmesan, to serve (optional)

1 Put the almonds, rosemary leaves and sun-dried tomatoes, along with the oil from the jar, into a food processor or blender and add the roasted red peppers, garlic and generous pinches of salt and pepper. Add the cream a little at a time and keep processing until smooth (if you're using a blender, you might need to add a little bit more cream so the sauce blends well).

2 Put a frying pan on a low heat and pour in the red sauce.

3 Meanwhile, cook the gnocchi in a large saucepan according to the packet instructions. Once they have floated to the surface, spoon them straight into the pan of sauce, adding a splash of the pasta water if needed to loosen it up, then stir everything together.

4 Finish with an extra pinch of pepper and serve with grated vegan Parmesan, if you like.

GLUTEN-FREE (USE GF GNOCCHI)

'NDUJA TOFU SCRAMBLE

Ben's vegan 'nduja paste is famous in our household. In non-vegan circles it's a spreadable and spicy pork sausage. In our world it's made using miso and sun-dried tomatoes, and we add it to pastas, pizzas or – like we do here – our silky tofu scramble for a fabulous brunch. If you fancy making a big batch, you can store the 'nduja paste in an airtight container in the fridge for up to 5 days.

EQUIPMENT: **FRYING PAN / MIXING BOWL**

SERVES **2** / PREP **10 MINS** / COOK **5 MINS**

450g silken tofu

½ tsp ground turmeric

salt + pepper

4 slices of crusty bread

a small handful of fresh
   parsley (10g), leaves
   picked

FOR THE 'NDUJA

30g sun-dried tomatoes
   in oil, drained + finely
   chopped, plus a little oil
   from the jar

1 garlic clove, peeled +
   finely chopped

½ a red chilli, finely
   chopped

1 tsp smoked paprika

½ tbsp red wine vinegar

2 tsp miso paste (we use
   white miso)

1 Drizzle a little oil from the jar of sun-dried tomatoes into a frying pan on a medium-high heat. Crumble the tofu between your fingers straight into the pan, then add the turmeric and generous pinches of salt and pepper. Fry for 5–10 minutes, or until hot and combined, breaking up the tofu with the back of a wooden spoon as you stir.

2 Meanwhile, put the sun-dried tomatoes, garlic and chilli (seeds removed if you don't like it hot) into a mixing bowl with the smoked paprika, vinegar, miso paste and a splash of the oil from the jar of sun-dried tomatoes. Stir until combined, to create a runny paste.

3 Toast the bread and serve on plates with the tofu scramble mixture. Top with the 'nduja and the parsley leaves.

GLUTEN-FREE (USE GF BREAD)
HIGH IN PROTEIN
ONE-PAN

CABBAGE TAHINI NOODLES

We try to use up whichever noodles we have lying around in the cupboard – wholewheat, soba or udon will all do fine. This speedy meal is perfect for midweek dinners when you're struggling for time. Sometimes we add fried tofu – cooked separately – for extra protein.

EQUIPMENT: FRYING PAN OR WOK / SAUCEPAN / SMALL BOWL

SERVES 3–4 / PREP 5 MINS / COOK 8 MINS

sesame oil

500g white cabbage, finely sliced

2 large carrots, sliced into matchsticks

4 garlic cloves, peeled + finely sliced

150g wheat noodles

1½ limes, juice only

3 tbsp dark soy sauce

4 tbsp tahini

1 tbsp maple syrup

3 spring onions, sliced lengthways

1 Heat a generous drizzle of sesame oil in a frying pan or wok on a high heat. Once hot, add the cabbage and carrots and fry for 3 minutes, then add the garlic and fry for 2 minutes.

2 Meanwhile, cook the noodles according to the packet instructions and drain them a minute before they are ready, reserving some of the cooking water.

3 In a small bowl combine the lime juice, soy sauce, tahini and maple syrup with 2 tablespoons of the noodle cooking water to make a smooth sauce (you may need to add more water if your tahini is thick).

4 Add the cooked noodles straight to the frying pan. Then add the tahini sauce and spring onions. Stir to combine, and serve with an extra drizzle of sesame oil.

GLUTEN-FREE (USE GF NOODLES + TAMARI)

KALE + ORANGE SALAD
WITH GINGER DRESSING

We love adding fresh ginger to our dressings. It totally elevates this fresh kale salad, which we enjoy either as a light meal or as part of a big spread. Don't forget you can also use the leftover kale stalks in your morning smoothie.

EQUIPMENT: LARGE MIXING BOWL / FRYING PAN / SMALL BOWL

SERVES 4 / PREP 10 MINS / COOK 5 MINS

350g kale, stalks removed
+ leaves chopped

2 tbsp apple cider vinegar

1½ tsp sesame oil,
plus extra

salt + pepper

120g pecans,
roughly chopped

120g raisins

½ a red onion, peeled +
thinly sliced

5 large oranges

a thumb of fresh
ginger (30g), peeled +
finely grated

1 tbsp maple syrup

1 Put the chopped kale leaves into a large mixing bowl along with 1 tablespoon of apple cider vinegar, ½ teaspoon of sesame oil and a pinch of salt. Massage the kale for 2 minutes, until it has softened and reduced in volume.

2 Put the pecans into a frying pan on a medium heat and toast for a few minutes, until fragrant, then add them to the kale along with the raisins and onion. Peel and slice 3 of the oranges and add them to the bowl.

3 Cut the remaining 2 oranges in half and squeeze the juice straight into a small bowl (you should have around 100ml of juice). Then add the ginger, maple syrup, the remaining 1 tablespoon of apple cider vinegar, pinches of salt and pepper and the remaining 1 teaspoon of sesame oil. Stir to combine, then pour the dressing all over the salad, gently mix with your hands and serve on a big plate.

GLUTEN-FREE
ONE-PAN

FIERY PEPPERCORN STIR-FRY

We're obsessed with adding lots of freshly ground black pepper to our stir-fry dishes. It's a staple ingredient that unlocks a wonderfully fiery flavour. Most extra firm tofu won't need pressing, but if your tofu is a little soft, we'd recommend first squeezing out as much water as possible.

EQUIPMENT: SAUCEPAN / NON-STICK WOK OR FRYING PAN

SERVES 2 / PREP 3 MINS / COOK 12 MINS

160g jasmine rice

2 tbsp cornflour

300g block of extra firm
   tofu, drained

sesame oil

3 garlic cloves, peeled +
   finely chopped

½ a red chilli, sliced

1 tbsp light soy sauce

2 tbsp hoisin sauce

2 spring onions, sliced

½ tbsp freshly ground
   black pepper

2 pak choi, halved
   lengthways

1 Cook the jasmine rice according to the packet instructions. Put the cornflour on a plate, then slice the tofu into bite-size chunks and coat them in the cornflour.

2 Pour a splash of sesame oil into a non-stick wok or frying pan on a medium-high heat and fry the tofu for 10 minutes, until golden and crispy on all sides.

3 Add a little more sesame oil to the pan, then add the garlic and red chilli and fry for 1 minute. Add the soy sauce, hoisin sauce, spring onions, black pepper and pak choi, along with 4 tablespoons of water. Stir and simmer for 1–2 minutes, or until the sauce has thickened slightly. Serve with the jasmine rice.

GLUTEN-FREE (USE TAMARI)
HIGH IN PROTEIN

SAUTÉD COURGETTE
WITH TOMATO BULGUR + SUMAC SALT

Bulgur wheat is a staple in the Middle East. It's made from a whole grain (the 'groats' are blanched, then crushed), so it's high in fibre and we're always using it to bulk out our meals. If you prefer, you can swap it for rice (just be sure to add less water and cook the rice with the lid on) – which will also make this recipe gluten-free.

EQUIPMENT: SAUCEPAN / LARGE FRYING PAN / 2 SMALL BOWLS

SERVES 4 / PREP 4 MINS / COOK 11 MINS

olive oil

2 tsp coriander seeds

2 tbsp tomato purée

300g bulgur wheat

2 garlic cloves, unpeeled

salt + pepper

2 courgettes, sliced into
   1cm rings

1 tbsp sumac

200g vegan yoghurt (we
   use oat Greek style)

a handful of fresh parsley
   (15g), roughly chopped

½ a lemon, sliced into
   6 wedges

1 Put 1 teaspoon of olive oil into a saucepan on a medium heat. Add the coriander seeds and cook for a minute or until they turn a darker brown, then turn the heat down and stir in the tomato purée, bulgur wheat, unpeeled garlic cloves, 600ml of hot water straight from a kettle and small pinches of salt and pepper. Gently simmer for 5 minutes, then turn off the heat, cover with a lid, pop a tea towel loosely on top and leave to steam cook for another 5 minutes.

2 Meanwhile, put 1 tablespoon of olive oil into a large frying pan on a medium-high heat. Add the courgettes, along with small pinches of salt and pepper, and cook for 8 minutes or until golden and slightly charred on both sides.

3 Combine the sumac with ½ teaspoon of salt in a small bowl, then set aside. When the bulgur is ready, take out the garlic cloves and remove their skins, then finely chop the garlic. Put the garlic into a separate small bowl, along with the yoghurt and most of the parsley. Squeeze the juice from 2 lemon wedges into the bowl of yoghurt, then stir to combine.

4 To serve, put the bulgur on plates with the garlic yoghurt and courgettes. Sprinkle over the sumac salt and the remaining parsley, and squeeze the rest of the lemon wedges all over.

GLUTEN-FREE (SWAP BULGUR FOR RICE)

MEXICAN LENTIL BOWL
WITH JALAPEÑO DRESSING

This is what speedy cooking is all about – a nutritious bowl filled with aromatic lentils, a spicy salsa and coconut yoghurt, which is ready in under 15 minutes. We use a ready-to-go fajita seasoning mix, but if you prefer, you can assemble your blend using ground cumin, ground coriander, smoked paprika, onion powder and chilli powder – simply taste and adjust the amounts to your liking!

EQUIPMENT: **FRYING PAN / SMALL BOWL**

SERVES **4** / PREP **5 MINS** / COOK **8 MINS**

olive oil

4 garlic cloves, peeled + sliced

2 x 250g pouches of cooked Puy lentils

2 tbsp fajita seasoning mix

½ tbsp dried oregano

160g frozen sweetcorn

salt + pepper

100g baby spinach

2 tbsp jarred sliced jalapeños, finely chopped

a bunch of fresh coriander (30g), finely chopped

1 lime, juice only

2 avocados, peeled + sliced

4 dollops of vegan yoghurt (we use coconut)

1 Heat a generous splash of oil in a frying pan on a medium-high heat. Once hot, fry the garlic for 2 minutes, then add the lentils, fajita seasoning, oregano, sweetcorn, generous pinches of salt and pepper and 120ml of water. Cook for 3 minutes, then throw in the spinach along with another splash of water and fry for 3–5 minutes, or until the spinach has wilted.

2 Put the jalapeños and coriander into a small bowl with the lime juice, 2 tablespoons of olive oil and pinches of salt and pepper, and stir to combine.

3 Serve the lentil mixture in bowls, top with the avocado slices, add a dollop of yoghurt and finish with a drizzle of the jalapeño salsa.

GLUTEN-FREE
ONE-PAN

DOUBLE CHEESE BEETROOT BURGERS

Cooked beetroot and chickpeas form the basis of these super simple vegan patties. They have a wonderfully light texture as well as a lovely warmth from the spices. Simply double or triple the quantities if you want to make a bigger batch – and build with your go-to toppings (we've suggested our favourites).

EQUIPMENT: MIXING BOWL / SMALL BOWL / LARGE NON-STICK FRYING PAN

SERVES 2 / PREP 7 MINS / COOK 8 MINS

½ x 400g tin of chickpeas, drained + rinsed

250g cooked beetroot (vacuum-packed), grated

½ a red onion, finely chopped

4 tbsp chickpea flour

½ tsp ground cumin

½ tsp smoked paprika

salt + pepper

olive oil

4 slices of vegan cheese

2 burger buns

optional toppings: mustard, gherkins, lettuce, vegan mayonnaise + ketchup

1 Put the chickpeas into a mixing bowl and mash until they're mostly broken down. In a separate small bowl, use your hands to squeeze as much liquid as possible out of the grated beetroot (if there's a lot of liquid, you can try using a clean tea towel to wring it out), then add the beetroot to the bowl of mashed chickpeas and discard the liquid.

2 Next go in with the onion, chickpea flour, spices and pinches of salt and pepper. Divide the mixture into four, then shape into round flat patties about 1½cm thick.

3 Heat a splash of olive oil in a large non-stick frying pan on a medium heat. Cook the patties for 4–5 minutes on each side, or until crispy and slightly charred. A minute or so before they're ready, add a slice of cheese to each patty and cover the pan with a lid. Cook until the cheese has softened, then start building your burgers with your favourite toppings.

4 We usually spoon some mustard on the bottom half of each bun, then add 2 patties to each half, followed by sliced gherkin, lettuce leaves, both vegan mayonnaise and ketchup, and top with the other half of the bun.

FREEZER-FRIENDLY (PATTIES ONLY)
GLUTEN-FREE (USE GF BUNS)
HIGH IN PROTEIN
ONE-PAN

MASALA TOFU + CARDAMOM RICE

Cardamom adds an incredible aroma to dishes, and for this quick and simple meal we add it towards the end of the cooking, to release its delicate fragrance. Another neat trick is using smoked tofu, which adds a whole new level to this wonderful and vibrant curried rice.

EQUIPMENT: **NON-STICK FRYING PAN / LARGE SAUCEPAN**

SERVES **2** / PREP **5 MINS** / COOK **10 MINS**

vegetable oil

300g block of extra firm tofu, drained (we use smoked tofu)

1 tsp garam masala

salt + pepper

½ a thumb of fresh ginger (15g), peeled + finely chopped

200g frozen peas

1 x 250g pouch of cooked basmati rice

2 spring onions, sliced

½ a vegetable stock cube

3 cardamom pods, seeds chopped or crushed

½ a lemon, zest + juice

a handful of fresh mint (15g), leaves picked

1 Put 1 tablespoon of vegetable oil into a non-stick frying pan on a medium-high heat. Tear the tofu into small chunks directly into the pan, then add the garam masala and pinches of salt and pepper. Fry for 8 minutes or until the tofu is crispy. Add the ginger and cook for another 2 minutes, then remove the pan from the heat and set to one side.

2 Meanwhile, cook the peas in a large saucepan of boiling water for 2 minutes, then drain and put the peas back into the saucepan. Add the cooked rice and spring onions. Dissolve the vegetable stock cube in a jug with 100ml of hot water, then add it to the saucepan along with the crushed cardamom seeds. Stir and heat through for 1–2 minutes.

3 Add the lemon zest and juice and fried tofu to the saucepan of rice. Tear in the mint leaves, then give it all a good stir and season to taste with more salt and pepper. Serve on plates and top with a pinch of the lemon zest.

GLUTEN-FREE
HIGH IN PROTEIN

CURRIED TOMATOES + CHICKPEAS ON TOAST

We love cooking with spices, and this recipe is the perfect example why. Toasting whole spices dry in a pan creates a more complex and bold flavour, which totally elevates the tomatoes and chickpeas. We often enjoy this versatile dish as a breakfast, lunch or dinner!

EQUIPMENT: **MIXING BOWL / FRYING PAN**

SERVES **2** / PREP **5 MINS** / COOK **10 MINS**

⅓ of a cucumber, diced

½ a red onion, peeled + finely chopped

1 lime, juice only

salt + pepper

1 tsp coriander seeds

1 tsp cumin seeds

olive oil

200g cherry tomatoes

2 garlic cloves, peeled + sliced

1 x 400g tin of chickpeas, drained + rinsed

2 tsp mango chutney

½ tsp ground turmeric

4 thick slices of bread

1 Put the cucumber, red onion, lime juice and a pinch of salt into a mixing bowl. Mix, then set aside for later.

2 Place a frying pan on a medium heat. When the pan is hot, add the coriander and cumin seeds. Toast in the dry pan for 2–3 minutes or until they turn a darker brown, then transfer them to a plate.

3 Add 1 tablespoon of olive oil to the same pan on a medium heat. Add the tomatoes and cook for 5–6 minutes, or until they begin to char. Add the garlic and cook for a minute.

4 Lower the heat, then slowly crush the tomatoes using a masher – just enough to release some of their juices (be careful of the hot juices when crushing). Return the toasted spices to the pan, along with the chickpeas, mango chutney, turmeric and pinches of salt and pepper. Stir, then add a splash of water to loosen the sauce and heat through for a minute.

5 Toast the bread, drizzle a small splash of olive oil over the toast and top with the curried tomatoes and chickpeas, followed by the cucumber and red onion.

GLUTEN-FREE (USE GF BREAD)

ONE-PAN

CHICKPEA 'TUNA' PASTA SALAD
WITH CHARRED SWEETCORN

This salad is a homage to the tuna pasta we ate growing up as kids. We use mashed chickpeas for their texture, along with capers, fresh dill and lemon for their salty and zingy flavour. Charred sweetcorn gives this salad an extra edge – the smoky kernels add a delicious dimension to this fresh and vibrant meal, and we use yoghurt as a healthier alternative to vegan mayo.

EQUIPMENT: SAUCEPAN / SMALL BOWL / FRYING PAN / MIXING BOWL

SERVES 4 / PREP 3 MINS / COOK 12 MINS

320g pasta (we use conchiglie)

½ a red onion, peeled + chopped

1 lemon, juice only

salt + pepper

olive oil

200g frozen sweetcorn

1 x 400g tin of chickpeas, drained + rinsed

1 tsp Dijon mustard

2 celery sticks, chopped

a handful of fresh dill (15g), roughly chopped

5 tbsp vegan yoghurt (we use oat Greek style)

2 tbsp capers, plus 2 tbsp caper juice

1 Cook the pasta according to the packet instructions, then drain, run it under cold water to cool it down and set aside. Combine the red onion, the juice of half the lemon and pinches of salt and pepper in a small bowl, and also set aside.

2 Put 2 teaspoons of olive oil into a frying pan on a medium-high heat. Toss in the sweetcorn and cook for 8–10 minutes, or until the sweetcorn is nicely charred. Watch out – some kernels might jump out of the pan as they heat up.

3 Put the chickpeas into a mixing bowl. Mash until almost all the chickpeas have broken down, then add the mustard, celery, dill, yoghurt, capers and caper juice. Stir, then add the cooked pasta, red onion, the juice from the remaining lemon half and the charred sweetcorn. Give it all another good stir and season to taste with salt and pepper.

4 To serve, drizzle over an extra splash of olive oil and black pepper.

GLUTEN-FREE (USE GF PASTA)

NUTTY SUPERFOOD SALAD

Most supermarkets now stock a wide array of 'ready to eat' cooked grains, which are sold in pouches and are often already seasoned with herbs and spices. They're ideal for speeding up your healthy lunches and dinners – such as this superfood salad, where we throw together a pouch of cooked red rice and quinoa with edamame and broccoli, then top with toasted nuts and a tahini dressing. Simple and delicious.

EQUIPMENT: SAUCEPAN / LARGE MIXING BOWL / FRYING PAN / SMALL BOWL

SERVES 4 / PREP 6 MINS / COOK 9 MINS

200g frozen edamame

olive oil

300g Tenderstem broccoli

salt + pepper

2 x 250g pouches of
   cooked mixed grains
   (we use red rice +
   quinoa)

a handful of fresh
   coriander (15g),
   roughly chopped

100g mixed nuts, roughly
   chopped (we use
   pistachios + almonds)

1 tbsp light soy sauce

1 lime, juice only

3 tbsp tahini

1½ tbsp maple syrup

1 Put the edamame into a saucepan of boiling water and cook for 3–4 minutes until al dente, then drain and place in a large mixing bowl. Heat a drizzle of oil in a frying pan on a medium-high heat. Slice any large broccoli in half lengthways, then add all the broccoli to the pan, sprinkle with generous pinches of salt and pepper, and fry for 4 minutes or until tender. Transfer the broccoli to the bowl of edamame, followed by the cooked mixed grains and coriander, and mix.

2 Wipe out the pan and toast the nuts for 2–3 minutes, until golden, then put them on a plate on the side. For the dressing, combine the soy sauce, lime juice, tahini and maple syrup in a small bowl. Add a splash of water a tablespoon at a time until the dressing is smooth and runny. Taste and adjust the amount of maple syrup to your liking.

3 Transfer the salad to a serving plate. Top with the toasted nuts, drizzle some of the dressing all over, and serve the rest of the dressing alongside.

GLUTEN-FREE (USE TAMARI)
HIGH IN PROTEIN

CHARRED ZA'ATAR CABBAGE
WITH LENTIL TABBOULEH

If you follow us on social media, you've probably heard us go on and on about our love for za'atar – a zesty and herby spice blend from the Middle East. Lately we've been using it almost exclusively as a condiment – at the end of cooking to coat our veggies, salads and breads. You'll now find it in most large supermarkets, but in our opinion it really does pay to find a good quality version from a specialist store. We usually enjoy this as a light lunch or serve it with crusty bread for dinner.

EQUIPMENT: **LARGE FRYING PAN / SAUCEPAN / MIXING BOWL**

SERVES **4** / PREP **8 MINS** / COOK **6 MINS**

1 Savoy cabbage

2 tbsp vegan butter or margarine

2 x 250g pouches of cooked Puy lentils

200g cherry tomatoes, halved

a bunch of fresh flat-leaf parsley (30g), roughly chopped

a bunch of fresh mint (30g), roughly chopped

1 lemon, juice only

olive oil

salt + pepper

2 tbsp za'atar

300g vegan yoghurt (we use oat Greek style)

1 Remove 1 or 2 outer leaves of the cabbage and slice through the centre into 8 wedges – keeping the core intact so that the wedges hold together. Put the vegan butter into a large frying pan on a medium-high heat. As soon as it has melted, add the wedges and cook for 3–4 minutes or until charred, then carefully turn and cook until charred on the other side. If necessary, cook the wedges using 2 pans or in batches (adding more butter, if required).

2 Meanwhile, put the lentils into a saucepan with a splash of water and heat through on a medium heat for 2–3 minutes, then transfer them to a mixing bowl. Add the tomatoes, parsley, mint, lemon juice, 3 tablespoons of olive oil and generous pinches of salt and pepper. Stir and set aside.

3 As soon as the cabbage wedges are nicely charred, transfer them to a chopping board. Sprinkle over 1½ tablespoons of the za'atar and – being careful not to break up the cabbage too much – coat the wedges with it.

4 To serve, divide the yoghurt among plates and top with the lentil tabbouleh and the charred cabbage (along with any za'atar from the bottom of the bowl). Sprinkle over the remaining za'atar and drizzle over some olive oil to finish.

GLUTEN-FREE
HIGH IN PROTEIN

OUR GO-TO LO MEIN

The sauce we use for these lo mein (aka stirred noodles) is a template we use all the time to cook delicious and speedy noodles at home. Practically everything else is up for grabs – throw in your leftover veggies and noodles, as well as fried tofu if you fancy it. We tend to use regular thin wheat noodles, but thicker (udon) or buckwheat (soba) will also work really well – and be sure to slice any chunkier veggies thinly enough so everything cooks evenly.

EQUIPMENT: **WOK OR FRYING PAN / SAUCEPAN**

SERVES **2** / PREP **5 MINS** / COOK **9 MINS**

50g cashews

160g wheat noodles

3 spring onions

200g crunchy veg
(we use mangetout,
baby corn + carrot)

1½ tsp sesame oil

½ a thumb of fresh ginger
(15g), peeled + finely
chopped

1 tbsp dark soy sauce

1 tbsp light soy sauce

1 tbsp maple syrup

1 tsp rice wine (we use
Shaoxing wine or mirin)

1 Put the cashews into a wok or frying pan on a medium heat and cook for a few minutes until brown and slightly charred, then transfer to a plate and set aside.

2 Meanwhile, bring a saucepan of water to the boil. Add the noodles and cook until slightly soft and still chewy, then drain and rinse under cold water to prevent them going soft.

3 Roughly chop the spring onions into large pieces and, if necessary, slice any of the large chunky vegetables such as baby corn and carrot. Wipe the wok with a clean tea towel, then return it to a medium-high heat and add 1 teaspoon of sesame oil. Add the spring onions and chunky vegetables and stir-fry for 2–3 minutes.

4 Next add the ginger, the remaining ½ teaspoon of sesame oil, the dark soy sauce, light soy sauce, maple syrup and rice wine. Cook for another minute, stirring regularly, until the sauce begins to reduce and thicken. Turn the heat down to medium, stir in the noodles and cashews, and heat through for 20–30 seconds, then serve.

GLUTEN-FREE (USE GF NOODLES, TAMARI + MIRIN)

GIANT COUSCOUS, LEEK + BROCCOLI

This is the type of meal we'll usually rustle up for lunch on a weekend or as a quick midweek dinner. It's wonderfully simple and captures lots of what we love about Mediterranean cuisine – salty olives, zesty lemon juice and the sharpness from the white wine. You can easily make this your own. Stir in tinned white beans at the end for extra protein or substitute broccoli with leafy greens such as kale or spinach.

EQUIPMENT: **SAUCEPAN / LARGE FRYING PAN**

SERVES **4** / PREP **5 MINS** / COOK **10 MINS**

300g giant couscous

olive oil

1 leek, sliced

1 broccoli

150ml vegan dry
   white wine

1 tsp fennel seeds

1 vegetable stock cube

½ a lemon, juice only

100g pitted Kalamata
   olives, halved

salt + pepper

100g vegan feta (optional)

1 Bring a saucepan of salted water to the boil. Add the couscous and cook for 8 minutes (the couscous should still be slightly chewy), then drain.

2 Meanwhile, drizzle some olive oil into a large frying pan on a medium-high heat. Add the leek and cook for 3 minutes. While the leek is cooking, break the broccoli head into florets, chop the florets into small pieces and dice the stem, then set aside. Turn up the heat a touch and pour the wine into the pan, then cook for 1–2 minutes, or until it has mostly reduced.

3 Add the chopped broccoli florets and stem to the pan, followed by the fennel seeds. Dissolve the stock cube in a jug with 200ml of hot water straight from a kettle and pour into the pan. Cook for 2–3 minutes, or until the broccoli is tender but still crunchy.

4 Remove the pan from the heat and add the cooked couscous, lemon juice and olives. Stir and season to taste with salt and pepper.

5 To serve, crumble over the vegan feta and top with olive oil and extra black pepper.

BROTHY KALE + CHICKPEA BOWL

It's genuinely hard to overplay just how satisfying this simple bowl of kale and chickpeas really is. What holds this perfect dish together is the miso broth, which is like a warm hug of deliciousness and is the ideal vessel for dunking our warm garlic butter baguette. Utterly divine.

EQUIPMENT: LARGE POT / GRIDDLE PAN OR LARGE BAKING TRAY / SMALL BOWL

SERVES 4 / PREP 5 MINS / COOK 10 MINS

3 tbsp vegan butter or margarine

1 onion, peeled + finely chopped

1 litre vegetable stock

2 tbsp miso paste (we use white miso)

150g chopped kale

2 x 400g tins of chickpeas, drained + rinsed

½ a large baguette, sliced

2 garlic cloves, peeled + finely chopped

salt + pepper

1 Melt 1 tablespoon of butter in a large pot on a medium heat and fry the onion for 5 minutes. Add the stock, miso paste, kale and chickpeas. Bring the broth to the boil, then reduce the heat and simmer for 5–6 minutes, until the kale is soft.

2 While the broth is simmering, toast the slices of baguette in a hot griddle pan or place them on a large baking tray and put them under the grill for 1–2 minutes on each side, or until golden.

3 Meanwhile, in a small bowl combine the remaining 2 tablespoons of butter with the garlic and a pinch of salt and pepper. Then spread the garlic butter all over the warm toasted bread.

4 Stir ½ teaspoon of freshly ground black pepper into the broth, and serve in bowls with slices of garlic bread. Top each bowl with extra black pepper to serve.

FREEZER-FRIENDLY

GLUTEN-FREE (USE GF BAGUETTE)

SPRING PANZANELLA

The truth is there's absolutely nothing wrong with the classic panzanella, a summer Italian salad traditionally made with ripe tomatoes. Well, that is apart from the fact that we usually can't wait until the summer to eat it, which is when we turn to this – a seasonal twist using asparagus but with all your panzanella favourites: stale bread, capers, cucumber and lots of fresh basil.

EQUIPMENT: **LARGE BAKING TRAY / FRYING PAN / SMALL BOWL / MIXING BOWL**

SERVES **3–4** / PREP **7 MINS** / COOK **8 MINS**

300g stale bread, cut
   into cubes

olive oil

salt + pepper

250g asparagus spears

4 tbsp red wine vinegar

2 tbsp capers, plus 1 tbsp
   caper juice

½ a cucumber, sliced into
   semicircles

3 spring onions, sliced

a large handful of fresh
   basil (20g), leaves
   picked + torn

1 Preheat the oven to 200°C fan/220°C/gas 7. Put the bread on a large baking tray and drizzle with olive oil. Sprinkle with salt and pepper and toss to combine, then bake for 8–10 minutes, or until the bread is golden.

2 Meanwhile, snap the woody ends off the asparagus and discard them, then slice the asparagus into 2½cm pieces, keeping the tips intact. Drizzle a little oil into a frying pan on a medium heat and fry the asparagus for 5 minutes.

3 In a small bowl combine the red wine vinegar with 60ml of oil, pinches of salt and pepper and 1 tablespoon of juice from the jar of capers.

4 Put the capers, cucumber, spring onions and basil into a mixing bowl along with the baked bread, asparagus and dressing. Stir to combine, then serve.

TANGY POPPADOM SALAD

One of the best things about eating at a South Asian restaurant is devouring the poppadoms and various condiments before the curry. For us, it's a real highlight of any curry night, and we capture that magical moment with this fuss-free and seriously flavoursome crunchy salad, which we top with tangy red onion and – of course – lime pickle.

EQUIPMENT: 2 SMALL BOWLS / FRYING PAN / MIXING BOWL

SERVES 4 / PREP 10 MINS / COOK 2 MINS

1 red onion, sliced

1 lemon, juice only

salt + pepper

1 tsp cumin seeds

2 tsp maple syrup

2 tbsp olive oil

1 x 400g tin of black
   beans, drained + rinsed

2 ripe tomatoes, chopped

60g poppadoms (6–7 small
   poppadoms)

60g salad leaves (we use
   lamb's lettuce)

2 tbsp lime pickle, to serve

1 Combine the red onion, the juice from half the lemon and a pinch of salt in a small bowl, then set aside.

2 Place a frying pan on a medium heat. When the pan is hot, add the cumin seeds and toast in the dry pan for 2–3 minutes, or until they turn a darker brown, then transfer them to a mixing bowl. Add the juice from the remaining lemon half, the maple syrup, olive oil and pinches of salt and pepper. Stir in the black beans and chopped tomatoes, then set aside.

3 To serve, break up a couple of the poppadoms and put them on a large serving plate with the salad leaves, then top with the black beans and tomatoes, followed by the pickled red onion. Put the lime pickle into a small bowl and loosen it with a splash of water, then spoon it over the salad and serve with the remaining poppadoms alongside.

SPINACH + SESAME SALAD

Toasting sesame seeds in a hot dry pan is a really simple method we use to introduce more flavour and texture into our meals. The toasted seeds add extra 'nuttiness' and crunch to this super easy salad, which combines a sweet and tangy sesame dressing, wilted spinach and crunchy veggies. We also use cooked quinoa, which is sold ready to eat – but you could easily switch this for other cooked grains, such as rice or barley.

EQUIPMENT: **FRYING PAN / SMALL BOWL**

SERVES **2** / PREP **5 MINS** / COOK **5 MINS**

3 tbsp sesame seeds

1 tsp sesame oil, plus extra

1½ tbsp light soy sauce

½ tbsp light brown sugar

1 tbsp rice vinegar

250g baby spinach

1 x 250g pouch of cooked quinoa

1 carrot, thinly sliced into matchsticks

3 spring onions, finely chopped

1 Heat a frying pan on a medium heat. Add the sesame seeds and toast in the dry pan for 2 minutes or until golden, then transfer them to a small bowl and combine with the sesame oil, soy sauce, sugar and rice vinegar. Set the sauce to one side for later.

2 Wipe out the frying pan, drizzle in a little sesame oil, then add the spinach and cook for 3–5 minutes, or until wilted. Remove the pan from the heat and stir in the cooked quinoa and the sesame sauce.

3 Divide the spinach and quinoa mixture between bowls, and top with the carrots and spring onions.

GLUTEN-FREE (USE TAMARI)

ONE-PAN

ONE-POT SUN-DRIED TOMATO ORZO

Despite what many traditionalists might think, one-pot pastas are officially here to stay – and we're totally on board with that. Our latest one-pot obsession is using orzo, which cooks perfectly into the sauce without breaking down. This dish is full of flavour, with olives, sun-dried tomatoes and basil all working together to deliver a comforting bowl of total yumminess in only 15 minutes.

EQUIPMENT: CASSEROLE POT OR HEAVY-BOTTOMED SAUCEPAN

SERVES 4 / PREP 3 MINS / COOK 12 MINS

olive oil

6 garlic cloves, peeled + finely sliced

2 x 400g tins of chopped tomatoes

120g pitted Kalamata olives, halved

1 tbsp red wine vinegar

450g orzo

salt + pepper

100g jarred sun-dried tomatoes, drained + sliced

a handful of fresh basil (15g), chopped

1 Drizzle a splash of olive oil into a casserole pot or heavy-bottomed saucepan on a medium heat. Add the garlic and fry for 2 minutes. Add the tinned tomatoes, then fill both empty tins to the top with water and pour it into the pot, followed by the olives, red wine vinegar, orzo and generous pinches of salt and pepper.

2 Stir, lower the heat, bring to a gentle simmer, then cover and cook for 10–12 minutes or until the orzo is al dente. Add more water if the sauce looks a little dry and the pasta still isn't cooked. Also, check on the pasta regularly and give it a good stir to prevent the orzo sticking to the bottom, which it can do.

3 When the orzo is cooked, stir in the sun-dried tomatoes and fresh basil, and serve with a drizzle of olive oil and some freshly ground black pepper.

FREEZER-FRIENDLY
GLUTEN-FREE (USE GF PASTA)
ONE-POT

CHIPOTLE MOLLETES

We're big believers in the open sandwich and they don't get much better than a mollete – a staple in Mexico City consisting of an open bread roll topped with refried beans and cheese. Our homage involves frying pinto beans with onion and chipotle paste for an intense smoky flavour. You can use whatever variety of vegan cheese you like – we usually go for a Cheddar style, which we find brings extra depth to the sandwich.

EQUIPMENT: **FRYING PAN / BAKING TRAY / MIXING BOWL**

SERVES **4** / PREP **5 MINS** / COOK **10 MINS**

olive oil

1½ small onions

2 x 400g tins of pinto beans, drained + rinsed

1 tbsp chipotle paste

salt + pepper

4 sandwich rolls

150g vegan cheese, grated (we use Cheddar style)

4 tomatoes

2 limes, juice only

a handful of fresh coriander (15g)

1 Heat a drizzle of oil in a frying pan on a medium-high heat. Peel and dice the half onion and fry for 3 minutes, until translucent. Add the beans, along with the chipotle paste, 120ml of water and generous pinches of salt and pepper. Stir, cook with the lid on for 5 minutes, then mash with a potato masher until thick. If it's loose, simmer for a couple more minutes, stirring constantly, until thickened.

2 Slice the sandwich rolls open, then divide the fried beans and spread across each half. Top each half with cheese and pop under the grill for 2–3 minutes, or until the cheese has melted.

3 Meanwhile, to make the salsa, chop the tomatoes, then peel and finely chop the remaining onion. Put both into a mixing bowl along with 2 tablespoons of olive oil, the lime juice and generous pinches of salt and pepper. Tear up the coriander and throw it into the bowl. Stir to combine.

4 Top the cheesy bread with the salsa and finish with a drizzle of oil and an extra sprinkling of salt and pepper.

BANG BANG GREENS

Bang bang sauce is an American invention that combines sweet chilli sauce, sriracha sauce and usually mayo to create an irresistibly creamy and spicy dressing (it's not to be confused with the Sichuan dish bang bang, which involves tenderizing meat!). For this speedy dish we drop the mayo and sub in peanut butter for a healthier and – in our opinion – even more irresistible sauce for our fried greens and noodles.

EQUIPMENT: MIXING BOWL / WOK OR LARGE FRYING PAN / SMALL BOWL

SERVES 3 / PREP 5 MINS / COOK 10 MINS

300g rice noodles

2 tsp sesame oil

1 broccoli, cut into small florets

100g fine green beans, trimmed

100g mangetout

1 tbsp light soy sauce

a handful of salted peanuts, roughly chopped

4 tbsp smooth peanut butter

2 tablespoons sweet chilli sauce

1 tablespoon sriracha sauce

1 teaspoon rice vinegar

1 Put the rice noodles into a mixing bowl, cover with boiling water straight from a kettle, set aside for 8–10 minutes to soften, then drain. The noodles should be soft but still slightly chewy.

2 Meanwhile, put the sesame oil into a wok or a large frying pan on a medium-high heat. Add the broccoli and green beans and cook for 3 minutes, or until they start to soften. Add the mangetout and cook for another 2 minutes, or until all the veggies are tender. Lower the heat, stir in the soy sauce and cook for 20–30 seconds, then remove the wok from the heat and top with the chopped peanuts.

3 Combine the peanut butter, sweet chilli sauce, sriracha and rice vinegar in a small bowl. Add a few splashes of water to loosen the sauce and serve alongside the noodles and stir-fried veggies.

GLUTEN-FREE (USE TAMARI)

HIGH IN PROTEIN

ONE-PAN

CHARRED CORN SALAD
WITH SWEET CHILLI DRESSING

Cooking the corn under the grill makes all the difference here. It adds a lovely charred flavour to the salad. Alternatively you can grill the corn on a barbecue if you want to make it extra special. This works brilliantly as a light lunch – you could serve it with tortilla crisps – or as a side.

EQUIPMENT: BAKING TRAY / SMALL BOWL / LARGE MIXING BOWL

SERVES **4** / PREP **5 MINS** / COOK **10 MINS**

2 corn ears

2 tbsp olive oil

salt + pepper

1 tsp paprika

200g red cabbage, finely sliced

a small handful of fresh basil (10g), leaves torn

1 cucumber, diced

3 limes

2 tbsp maple syrup

1 red chilli, finely chopped

1 Prepare the corn by removing any outer leaves, then place on a baking tray.

2 In a small bowl combine the olive oil with generous pinches of salt and pepper and the paprika, then brush this mixture all over the corn. Place the corn under a grill on a high setting for 10–12 minutes, or until the kernels are slightly charred, rotating every few minutes so it cooks evenly.

3 Meanwhile, put the cabbage, basil and cucumber into a large mixing bowl. Put the zest from half a lime and the juice from all 3 limes into a small bowl, and add the maple syrup and the finely chopped chilli (seeds removed if you don't like it hot). Pour the dressing over the cabbage salad and toss through.

4 Once the corn is ready, hold it in a tea towel and slice off the kernels. Add them to the mixing bowl, then toss the salad and serve.

GLUTEN-FREE
ONE-TRAY

FIESTA RICE

Fried rice is something that's almost always on rotation in our home, and it takes various forms from yang chow (Chinese) to pulao (Indian). But perhaps our favourite version uses chipotle paste for a smoky and spicy 'fiesta' of flavours. Occasionally we'll cook rice in advance, ready to stir into the pan. But when we're pushed for time, we'll just throw in a couple of ready-to-eat pouches of cooked rice – like we do here – for a super quick midweek dinner.

EQUIPMENT: CASSEROLE POT OR SAUCEPAN

SERVES 3 / PREP 4 MINS / COOK 11 MINS

olive oil

1 onion, peeled + finely chopped

3 garlic cloves, peeled + sliced

1 green pepper, diced

2 tsp chipotle paste

2 tbsp tomato purée

2 x 250g pouches of cooked wholegrain rice

2 x 400g tins of kidney beans, drained + rinsed

a bunch of fresh coriander (30g), chopped

½ a lemon, juice only

2 spring onions, sliced

salt

1 Drizzle some olive oil into a casserole pot or saucepan on a medium-high heat. Add the onion and garlic and cook for 5–6 minutes, or until brown. Add the green pepper and cook for 2 minutes.

2 Lower the heat a touch, then add the chipotle paste and tomato purée, along with a tablespoon of water to help loosen the pastes. Stir and cook for a minute, then add the rice, kidney beans and a few more tablespoons of water. Stir well and cook for a few minutes.

3 Finally, stir in the coriander, lemon juice and spring onions, season to taste with salt, and heat through for about 30 seconds before serving.

GLUTEN-FREE
ONE-POT

CRUNCHY PITTA + HUMMUS NACHOS

Hummus is arguably the greatest of all dips, and we give it the full treatment with these fully loaded pitta nachos. It's a great dish to bring out for barbecues or summer parties when you want a fresh and lighter take on nachos but something that's just as fun and delicious.

EQUIPMENT: **LARGE BAKING TRAY / FOOD PROCESSOR / SMALL BOWL**

SERVES **6** / PREP **10 MINS** / COOK **5 MINS**

6 white pittas

olive oil

salt + pepper

3 garlic cloves, unpeeled

1 x 400g tin of chickpeas,
  drained + rinsed

3 tbsp tahini

1 lemon

a large handful of fresh mint
  (20g), leaves picked

200g vegan yoghurt (we use
  oat Greek style)

$\frac{2}{3}$ of a cucumber, diced

100g jarred roasted red
  peppers, drained +
  chopped

80g pitted black olives,
  halved

sesame seeds, to serve
  (optional)

1 Preheat the oven to 200°C fan/220°C/gas 7. Slice the pittas into triangles like tortilla crisps, then spread them out on a large baking tray. Drizzle with olive oil and season with a pinch of salt and pepper, then scatter the unpeeled garlic cloves on the tray and bake for 5–10 minutes, or until the pitta crisps are golden, turning them over halfway through so they cook evenly.

2 Meanwhile, put the chickpeas, tahini, the juice of half the lemon and pinches of salt and pepper into a food processor. When the pitta crisps and garlic are ready, remove the cloves from the tray, peel off the skins and add them to the food processor. Process until everything is mostly broken down, then – while everything is blending – slowly pour in 4–6 tablespoons of cold water and keep processing until the hummus is lovely and smooth. If necessary, add more water to get the right consistency, then set aside.

3 Roughly chop half the mint leaves, then combine them in a small bowl with the yoghurt and half the cucumber to create your tzatziki.

4 To serve, put the pitta crisps on a large serving plate and top with dollops of the hummus, followed by the rest of the cucumber, the red peppers, olives, the tzatziki and the rest of the mint leaves. Sprinkle over some sesame seeds, then slice the remaining lemon half into wedges, add to the plate, and serve.

GLUTEN-FREE (USE GF PITTAS)
ONE-TRAY

15–30 MINS

SWEET POTATO KATSU

Katsu curry is one of those meals it's easy to get excited about. However, it can sometimes be quite complicated to cook at home, so for this simplified version we roast rings of sweet potato and serve them with a homemade katsu sauce, fluffy rice and a crunchy panko crumb.

EQUIPMENT: **LARGE BAKING TRAY / BAKING PAPER / SAUCEPAN / 2 FRYING PANS / BLENDER**

SERVES **4** / PREP **8 MINS** / COOK **20 MINS**

600g sweet potatoes, sliced into 1cm thick rings

vegetable oil

salt + pepper

250g jasmine rice

1 onion, peeled + chopped

2 carrots, diced into small pieces

6 garlic cloves, peeled + chopped

1 tbsp medium curry powder

1 x 400ml tin of coconut milk

1 tbsp maple syrup

40g panko breadcrumbs

2 spring onions, finely sliced

1 Preheat the oven to 200°C fan/220°C/gas 7 and line a large baking tray with baking paper. Place the sweet potatoes on the tray, drizzle with oil and sprinkle with pinches of salt and pepper. Toss, then roast for 20–25 minutes, or until soft.

2 Meanwhile, cook the rice according to the packet instructions. While the rice is cooking, heat a drizzle of oil in a frying pan on a medium heat. Fry the onion, carrot and two-thirds of the garlic for 8 minutes, then add the curry powder and a pinch of salt and fry for 1 minute. Stir in the coconut milk and maple syrup and simmer for 5 minutes, then remove the sauce from the heat and blend until smooth.

3 Drizzle a little oil into a separate frying pan and add the remaining garlic along with the panko and pinches of salt and pepper. Fry for 3 minutes or until the panko is golden, stirring constantly to prevent burning.

4 To serve, place a portion of rice on each serving plate, along with some katsu sauce and sweet potato. Sprinkle over the toasted panko and finish with the spring onions.

GLUTEN-FREE (USE GF BREADCRUMBS)

SWEET POTATO + CAULIFLOWER CHAAT

Chaat is a classic South Asian street food snack that usually includes fried dough. Our one-tray version switches it up with veggies for a healthier twist, without compromising the delicious spicy flavour.

EQUIPMENT: **LARGE ROASTING TRAY / SMALL BOWL / FOOD PROCESSOR OR PESTLE AND MORTAR**

SERVES **3–4** / PREP **5 MINS** / COOK **25 MINS**

800g sweet potato, diced

1 large cauliflower, cut into florets, leaves reserved

vegetable oil

salt + pepper

1 tbsp garam masala

1 tsp chilli powder

1 tsp fennel seeds

1 tsp ground ginger

250ml vegan yoghurt (we use oat)

1 tbsp maple syrup

½ a pomegranate

FOR THE GREEN DRESSING

a bunch of fresh coriander (30g)

½ tsp garam masala

2 green chillies (remove the seeds)

2 limes, juice only

3 garlic cloves, peeled

salt + pepper

1 Preheat the oven to 200°C fan/220°C/gas 7. Put the sweet potato, cauliflower florets and cauliflower leaves into a large roasting tray, drizzle with vegetable oil, sprinkle with salt and pepper and add the garam masala, chilli powder, fennel seeds and ground ginger. Toss until evenly coated, then bake for 10 minutes. Remove the leaves and set aside, then return the tray to the oven for another 15–20 minutes or until the vegetables are charred.

2 Meanwhile, in a small bowl combine the yoghurt and maple syrup and set to one side.

3 To make the green dressing, put most of the coriander (stalks and all, but save some leaves to top with later), the garam masala, chillies, lime juice, garlic and pinches of salt and pepper into either a food processor or a pestle and mortar. Process or pound to a smooth and runny consistency.

4 To serve, top the roasted veggies with the cauliflower leaves from earlier, along with the seeds from the pomegranate half and the rest of the coriander leaves. Drizzle over some of the yoghurt and green dressing and serve the rest alongside.

CREAMY PASTA E FAGIOLI

Pasta e fagioli, aka pasta and beans, is a traditional Italian pasta soup. Our version is less of a soup and more of a pasta. We parcook our farfalle, then add it to the sauce so that the remaining starch enhances the creamy texture. This is one of those meals that never fails to cheer us up.

EQUIPMENT: **FRYING PAN / SAUCEPAN**

SERVES **4** / PREP **10 MINS** / COOK **16 MINS**

100g walnuts, finely
   chopped

1 tsp chilli flakes

3 sprigs of fresh rosemary,
   leaves picked + finely
   chopped

salt + pepper

olive oil

1 leek, sliced

4 garlic cloves, peeled +
   finely sliced

1 x 400g tin of cannellini
   beans, drained + rinsed

250ml vegan cream (we
   use oat)

340g pasta (we use
   farfalle)

½ a lemon, juice only

1 Place a frying pan over a medium heat. When the pan is hot, add the walnuts along with ½ teaspoon of chilli flakes, two-thirds of the rosemary leaves and generous pinches of salt and pepper. Toast for 3–5 minutes, until the walnuts are golden. Then transfer this walnut crumb to a plate and save for later.

2 Wipe out the frying pan and add a generous drizzle of olive oil. Add the leek, garlic and the remaining ½ teaspoon of chilli flakes and fry for 3 minutes. Then add the cannellini beans, cream and the rest of the rosemary, and heat through for 5 minutes. Use the back of a wooden spoon to mash up half the beans to thicken the sauce.

3 Meanwhile, bring a pan of salted water to the boil, add the pasta and cook for 6–7 minutes.

4 Use a slotted spoon to transfer the pasta straight into the sauce, adding some of the pasta water as you go to loosen it. Simmer for 5 minutes, or until the sauce thickens and the pasta is al dente. Stir in the lemon juice and season to taste with salt and pepper.

5 To serve, sprinkle the walnut crumb all over and finish with a drizzle of olive oil and a sprinkling of cracked black pepper.

FREEZER-FRIENDLY (WITHOUT WALNUT CRUMB)

GLUTEN-FREE (USE GF PASTA)

RED PEPPER TAPENADE BAGUETTE PIZZAS

Ben has fond memories of making baguette pizzas at home as a kid. Here we take things up a few levels, with a homemade tapenade and a delicious almond ricotta. If you can't find demi baguettes, you can use a regular-sized baguette sliced in half.

EQUIPMENT: **SMALL BOWL** / **FOOD PROCESSOR** / **BAKING TRAY**

SERVES **4** / PREP **15 MINS** / COOK **8 MINS**

80g blanched almonds

200g jarred roasted red peppers, drained

120g pitted olives (we use black + green)

a bunch of fresh parsley (30g), plus extra

2 garlic cloves, peeled

2 tbsp lemon juice

olive oil

2 demi baguettes

2 tbsp nutritional yeast

100ml plant-based milk (we use oat)

salt + pepper

1 Put the almonds into a small bowl, cover with hot water from a kettle and leave to soak. Preheat the oven to 200°C fan/220°C/gas 7.

2 For the tapenade, put the roasted red peppers, most of the olives (saving a few to top with later), the parsley, garlic, lemon juice and 2 tablespoons of olive oil into a food processor and process until mostly broken down. Cut the baguettes in half lengthways and place them cut side up on a large baking tray. Spread the tapenade across the 4 baguette halves.

3 Wipe out the food processor and drain the almonds. To make the vegan ricotta, put the almonds into the processor along with the nutritional yeast, plant-based milk and pinches of salt and pepper, and process for a few minutes until smooth and creamy. If the ricotta is too lumpy, add some more plant-based milk 2 teaspoons at a time and process again until smooth.

4 Dollop the ricotta over the baguettes and bake for 8–10 minutes, until the edges of the baguettes turn golden.

5 To finish, slice the remaining olives into rings and sprinkle them over the baguettes, along with some black pepper, a drizzle of olive oil and a few parsley leaves.

GLUTEN-FREE (USE GF BAGUETTES)

ONE-TRAY

CORONATION CAULIFLOWER CIABATTA

Right now sandwiches are experiencing a renaissance, and rightly so. Sometimes only a sarnie will cut it, and this coronation cauliflower ciabatta hits all the spots – spiced and roasted florets mixed with a creamy and sweet sauce. Instead of discarding the cauliflower leaves, season and roast them with a touch of olive oil, then add to your soups before blending.

EQUIPMENT: **BAKING TRAY / LARGE MIXING BOWL**

SERVES **2** / PREP **8 MINS** / COOK **22 MINS**

½ a large cauliflower, cut into small florets, leaves removed

3 tsp medium curry powder

½ tsp smoked paprika

salt + pepper

vegetable oil

3 tbsp vegan mayonnaise

4 tbsp vegan yoghurt (we use oat)

½ tbsp mango chutney

1 tbsp raisins

2 ciabatta rolls

1 large tomato, sliced

a handful of green salad leaves

1 Preheat the oven to 200°C fan/220°C/gas 7. Put the cauliflower florets on a baking tray and toss with 2 teaspoons of the curry powder, the paprika, generous pinches of salt and pepper and a drizzle of oil. Roast for 15–20 minutes, until golden and cooked through, then remove from the oven and leave to cool.

2 Meanwhile, in a large mixing bowl combine the mayonnaise, yoghurt, chutney and raisins along with the remaining 1 teaspoon of curry powder and pinches of salt and pepper. Stir the cooled cauliflower into the sauce.

3 Cut the ciabatta rolls in half. Layer slices of tomato on each bottom half, then divide the Coronation cauliflower between the 2 rolls, and top with salad leaves. Cover with the top halves of the rolls and serve.

GLUTEN-FREE (USE GF ROLLS)

ONE-TRAY

SPINACH + ARTICHOKE PASTA

Don't hold back on the garlic here. Combined with the rosemary, it adds a distinctive nutty and earthy character to the tasty creamy pasta. This pasta will keep for 2–3 days in the fridge if you store it in an airtight container, so it's a great option for lunch during the week.

EQUIPMENT: **SAUCEPAN / FRYING PAN**

SERVES **4** / PREP **10 MINS** / COOK **12 MINS**

320g pasta (we use fusilli)

olive oil

6 garlic cloves, peeled + finely sliced

2 sprigs of fresh rosemary, leaves picked + chopped

1 tbsp plain flour

380ml plant-based milk (we use oat)

½ a vegetable stock cube

120g baby spinach

1 lemon, zest + juice

150g jarred artichokes, quartered

salt + pepper

1 Cook the pasta according to the packet instructions until al dente. Meanwhile, drizzle a little oil into a frying pan on a medium heat and fry the garlic and rosemary for 2 minutes. Add the flour, stir until combined, and cook for 30 seconds.

2 Slowly pour the plant-based milk into the pan, stirring continuously, then crumble in the stock cube half. Bring the sauce to a gentle simmer and cook for 5 minutes, until thickened, stirring occasionally.

3 Add the spinach and cook for 2–3 minutes, until wilted. Then use a slotted spoon to transfer the pasta straight into the sauce, adding some of the pasta water as you go to loosen it. Stir in the lemon juice and the artichokes, season to taste with salt and pepper, and top with lemon zest to serve.

FREEZER-FRIENDLY

GLUTEN-FREE (USE GF PASTA + FLOUR)

'SALMON' CARROT + MISO BUTTER ON TOAST

Before we were vegan, we'd never have imagined we'd be eating 'salmon' carrot, let alone on top of a rich miso butter spread over crusty bread. We use white miso here because it has a sweeter and more subtle flavour, but really any miso will do.

EQUIPMENT: **LARGE MIXING BOWL / SMALL BOWL**

SERVES **2** / PREP **20 MINS** / COOK **0 MINS**

2 carrots

½ tbsp capers, plus

 1½ tbsp caper juice

1 tbsp olive oil

1½ tbsp lemon juice

a handful of fresh dill (15g),

 chopped

salt + pepper

4 slices of sourdough

 bread

1 avocado, peeled + sliced

a handful of green salad

 leaves

FOR THE MISO BUTTER

3 tbsp vegan butter or

 margarine

1 tsp miso paste (we use

 white miso)

1 small garlic clove, peeled

 + finely chopped

1 Peel the carrots into ribbons and put them into a large mixing bowl with the capers, caper juice, olive oil, lemon juice, most of the chopped dill and pinches of salt and pepper. Give everything a stir and leave to one side to marinate for 15 minutes.

2 Meanwhile, in a small bowl combine the ingredients for the miso butter with the rest of the chopped dill.

3 To build the sandwiches, spread the 4 slices of bread with the miso butter. Lift the carrot from the marinade and gently squeeze out any excess liquid. Pile the carrot on to the buttered bread slices, then top with the avocado and salad leaves, and serve.

GLUTEN-FREE (USE GF BREAD)

COCONUT, CHILLI + LIME AUBERGINE CURRY

This aromatic one-pan curry is one of our go-to freezer-friendly meals. It'll keep well for a good 2–3 months. The sweet aromatic coconut sauce works brilliantly with the subtle flavour of the aubergine.

EQUIPMENT: **FRYING PAN**

SERVES **4** / PREP **5 MINS** / COOK **25 MINS**

vegetable oil

1 onion, peeled + finely sliced

2 aubergines, diced

salt + pepper

a handful of fresh coriander (15g)

4 red chillies

3 garlic cloves, peeled + finely chopped

a thumb of fresh ginger (30g), peeled + finely chopped

1 tsp garam masala

½ tsp ground fenugreek

1 x 400ml tin of coconut milk

2 tbsp tomato purée

½ a lime, juice only

4 naans

1 Heat a generous drizzle of oil in a large frying pan on a medium-high heat. Add the onion and fry for 3 minutes. Then add the aubergines along with an extra drizzle of oil and a pinch of salt, and fry for 10 minutes, or until soft.

2 Roughly chop the coriander stalks, pierce the red chillies a couple of times, then add both to the frying pan with the garlic, ginger, garam masala and fenugreek and fry for 2 minutes.

3 Pour in the coconut milk along with half a tin of water and the tomato purée. Stir, then simmer for 10–12 minutes until the sauce has thickened.

4 To finish, stir in the juice from the lime half and season to taste with salt and pepper. Top with the coriander leaves.

5 Heat the naans in a toaster and serve with the curry.

FREEZER-FRIENDLY (WITHOUT NAANS)
GLUTEN-FREE (USE GF NAANS)
ONE-PAN

BUFFALO CHICKPEA LETTUCE LEAF TACOS

Buffalo sauce is traditionally made using butter, but here we happily make do without for a slightly healthier and lighter twist to these lettuce tacos. If you're looking for ways to use the leftover juice from the tin of chickpeas, check out our delicious meringues on page 194.

EQUIPMENT: **ROASTING TRAY** / **LARGE MIXING BOWL** / **SMALL BOWL**

SERVES **4** / PREP **5 MINS** / COOK **23 MINS**

2 x 400g tins of chickpeas, drained + rinsed

olive oil

salt + pepper

100g red cabbage, coarsely grated

1 lemon, juice only

3 tbsp vegan mayonnaise

a small handful of fresh dill (10g), finely chopped, plus extra

3 tbsp hot sauce

1–2 little gem lettuces, leaves picked + rinsed

1 Preheat the oven to 200°C fan/220°C/gas 7. Put the chickpeas into a large roasting tray, drizzle with olive oil and sprinkle with salt. Roast for 20 minutes.

2 Meanwhile, put the red cabbage into a large mixing bowl with the juice from half the lemon and small pinches of salt and pepper. Toss and leave to one side to pickle.

3 For the dressing, in a small bowl combine the vegan mayonnaise, dill and a squeeze of juice from the remaining half lemon, enough to loosen up the dressing.

4 Remove the chickpeas from the oven and pour the hot sauce all over them. Stir to combine, then return the chickpeas to the oven for another 3 minutes.

5 Divide the chickpea mixture among the lettuce leaves, top with the pickled red cabbage and the mayo dressing, and finish with some extra sprinkles of dill.

GLUTEN-FREE
ONE-TRAY

TOFU LAHMACUN

Lahmacun is a staple in Turkey, Lebanon and Syria. Affectionately known as Middle Eastern pizza, it's usually made using minced meat, but we use crumbled tofu cooked with soy sauce and delicious spices.

EQUIPMENT: **SMALL BOWL / NON-STICK FRYING PAN / FRYING PAN**

SERVES **4** / PREP **15 MINS** / COOK **12 MINS**

1½ red onions

1½ lemons

3 tbsp pine nuts

olive oil

3 garlic cloves, peeled + finely chopped

400g block of extra firm tofu, drained

3 tbsp dark soy sauce

½ tsp ground cinnamon

½ tsp ground allspice

1½ tsp paprika

6 tbsp vegan yoghurt (we use oat)

2 tbsp tahini

4 flatbreads

a small handful of fresh mint (10g), leaves picked

1 Peel and thinly slice the half onion and put the slices into a small bowl with the juice from the half lemon. Toss and leave to one side to pickle.

2 Heat a non-stick frying pan on a medium heat. Add the pine nuts and toast for 2–3 minutes, or until golden, then remove them from the pan and leave to one side.

3 Peel and finely chop the remaining onion. Drizzle a little oil into the pan, then add the onion and fry for 4 minutes. Add the garlic and fry for 1 minute.

4 Squeeze out and discard any excess water from the tofu, then crumble it between your fingers straight into the pan and add the soy sauce, cinnamon, allspice and paprika. Fry for 5 minutes, breaking down the tofu even more with the back of a wooden spoon.

5 Meanwhile, combine the juice from half the remaining lemon with the yoghurt and tahini to make the dressing.

6 Heat the flatbreads in a hot frying pan, then transfer them to a plate. Spread a little tahini dressing over each one, then add the crumbled tofu mixture and drizzle with the rest of the dressing. Top with the toasted pine nuts, a few mint leaves and the pickled red onion. Cut the remaining half lemon into wedges and serve alongside the lahmacun flatbreads.

GLUTEN-FREE (USE GF FLATBREADS + TAMARI)

HIGH IN PROTEIN

HARISSA AUBERGINE ON BUTTER BEAN MASH

Nowadays you'll find rose harissa paste in most large supermarkets. It's slightly milder than regular harissa paste, and we use it for everything from Stuffed Courgettes (page 136) to Bolognese (page 158) – and to make this absolutely glorious aubergine dish.

EQUIPMENT: **SAUCEPAN / SMALL SAUCEPAN**

SERVES **3–4** / PREP **6 MINS** / COOK **24 MINS**

olive oil

2 aubergines, diced

1 onion, peeled + finely
    chopped

3 garlic cloves, peeled +
    finely chopped

1 tsp ground cinnamon

1 sprig of fresh rosemary,
    leaves picked +
    chopped

2 tbsp rose harissa paste

2 x 400g tins of green
    lentils, drained + rinsed

1 x 400g tin of chopped
    tomatoes

salt + pepper

a small handful of fresh
    parsley (10g), chopped

FOR THE MASH

2 x 400g tins of butter
    beans, drained + rinsed

1 lemon, juice only

1 Heat a drizzle of oil in a saucepan on a medium-high heat. Add the aubergines and fry for 8–10 minutes. Remove the aubergines from the pan, add the onion and an extra drizzle of oil, if necessary, and fry for 5 minutes.

2 Add the garlic, cinnamon and rosemary and fry for 1 minute. Stir in the rose harissa paste, lentils, chopped tomatoes and generous pinches of salt and pepper. Put the aubergines back into the pan, bring the mixture to the boil, then reduce the heat and simmer for 10 minutes.

3 Meanwhile, put the butter beans into a separate small saucepan on a medium heat. Add a drizzle of oil, pinches of salt and pepper, and the juice of the lemon. Heat the beans and mash with a masher until smooth.

4 Serve the aubergine and lentil mixture over the butter bean mash and finish with a drizzle of oil and the parsley.

FREEZER-FRIENDLY (AUBERGINE ONLY)

GLUTEN-FREE

CHEAT'S HOT + SOUR SOUP

Hot and sour soup is a popular dish from Sichuan province in China (where it's called suan la tang). Our simplified version uses easy-to-find ingredients that still pack the classic tangy and spicy flavours. And if bamboo's not your thing, simply switch it for a few handfuls of bean sprouts.

EQUIPMENT: **WOK OR LARGE SAUCEPAN / SAUCEPAN**

SERVES **4** / PREP **10 MINS** / COOK **15 MINS**

sesame oil

250g chestnut mushrooms, sliced into thick chunks

400g wheat noodles

1 red chilli, half finely diced + half sliced into rings (remove the seeds)

2 garlic cloves, peeled + finely chopped

a thumb of fresh ginger (30g), peeled + finely chopped

2½ tbsp dark soy sauce

4 tbsp apple cider vinegar

1 tbsp maple syrup

500ml low-sodium vegetable stock

1 x 225g tin of bamboo shoots, drained + rinsed

300g block of extra firm tofu, cut into cubes

2 spring onions, sliced

1 Drizzle a generous amount of sesame oil into a wok or large saucepan on a high heat and fry the mushrooms for 8 minutes.

2 Meanwhile, cook the noodles according to the packet instructions until al dente, then drain.

3 Add the diced chilli to the pan along with the garlic and ginger and fry for 2 minutes. Stir in the soy sauce, vinegar and maple syrup and cook for 1 minute.

4 Pour in the stock, along with 300ml of hot water straight from a kettle, then leave the soup to simmer for 2 minutes.

5 Add the cooked noodles, bamboo shoots and tofu and heat through for a few minutes.

6 Sprinkle the sliced chilli over the top of the soup, together with the spring onions, and serve.

FREEZER-FRIENDLY (WITHOUT NOODLES)

GLUTEN-FREE (USE GF NOODLES + TAMARI)

PORTOBELLO STEAKS + MASH

We're big believers that vegan cooking really doesn't have to be complicated to get amazing results. Often our favourite recipes are those using ingredients as they come – such as these portobello mushrooms, which we roast with rosemary until they're perfectly juicy. Be sure to use whole peppercorns and crush them yourself to capture all their flavour.

EQUIPMENT: **LARGE BAKING TRAY** / **PESTLE AND MORTAR** / **SMALL BOWL** / **LARGE SAUCEPAN** / **FRYING PAN**

SERVES **4** / PREP **7 MINS** / COOK **23 MINS**

750g portobello or large
   flat mushrooms
2 tsp black peppercorns
2 sprigs of fresh rosemary,
   leaves picked + finely
   chopped
3 tbsp vegan butter or
   margarine
2 tbsp light soy sauce
1kg potatoes, peeled +
   cut into 2–3cm chunks
salt
300ml vegan cream
   (we use oat)
200g asparagus spears
3 garlic cloves, peeled +
   finely chopped

1 Preheat the oven to 200°C fan/220°C/gas 7. Put the mushrooms on a large baking tray, stem side up. Use a pestle and mortar to coarsely crush the peppercorns (or put them into a plastic food bag and crush them with a rolling pin). Put a pinch of the crushed peppercorns into a small bowl with the rosemary, 1 tablespoon of butter and the soy sauce, stir to combine, and brush over the gills of the mushrooms. Roast for 15 minutes.

2 Meanwhile, put the potatoes into a large saucepan of boiling water and boil for 15 minutes, or until soft. Drain and leave to steam for a few minutes, then put them back into the saucepan. Add 1 tablespoon of butter, a pinch of salt and a pinch of the coarsely crushed peppercorns. Mash, then add a third of the cream and keep mashing until smooth.

3 Snap the woody ends off the asparagus and discard them, then add the asparagus to the tray of mushrooms and use any juice from the mushrooms in the tray to coat the asparagus. Roast everything for 8 minutes, or until the asparagus is tender but still has a crunch.

4 Put the remaining 1 tablespoon of butter into a frying pan on a medium heat. As soon as it has melted, add the garlic and fry for 1–2 minutes or until it begins to brown, then add the remaining cream and crushed black peppercorns, along with a pinch of salt. Stir and heat through for a minute or two, then remove from the heat.

5 Serve the mashed potato on plates, along with the mushrooms and asparagus, and pour over the creamy peppercorn sauce.

GLUTEN-FREE (USE TAMARI)

TERIYAKI MEATBALL RAMEN

This wonderful ramen isn't exactly conventional, but trust us when we say it's everything you want from a comforting bowl of noodles. We use regular wheat noodles, but practically any variety will do. You can also swap the almond butter for peanut butter or tahini.

EQUIPMENT: FOOD PROCESSOR / BAKING TRAY / BAKING PAPER / LARGE SAUCEPAN / SMALL BOWL

SERVES **4** / PREP **13 MINS** / COOK **17 MINS**

2 x 400g tins of black beans, drained + rinsed

a thumb of fresh ginger (30g), peeled + finely chopped

50g oats

60g walnuts

30g breadcrumbs (we use panko)

1 tsp sesame oil

3 tbsp teriyaki sauce

200g wheat noodles

3 tbsp miso paste (we use brown rice miso)

3 tbsp almond butter

1 litre vegetable stock

2 pak choi, leaves separated + rinsed

3 spring onions, sliced

1 Preheat the oven to 200°C fan/220°C/gas 7. Put the beans, ginger, oats, walnuts, breadcrumbs, sesame oil and 1 tablespoon of teriyaki sauce into a food processor. Pulse until the ingredients have mostly broken down and the mixture comes together in your hands, but avoid over-mixing.

2 Shape the mixture into 16 balls and put them on a baking tray lined with baking paper. Cook for 15 minutes in the oven, then brush the remaining 2 tablespoons of teriyaki sauce over the balls and cook for another 2 minutes.

3 Meanwhile, cook the noodles in a large saucepan of hot water until al dente, then drain under cold water and set aside.

4 Combine the miso paste, almond butter and 200ml of water in a small bowl so you have a smooth pourable liquid, and set aside.

5 Using the same pan you used to cook the noodles, pour in the vegetable stock and top up with another 500ml of hot water straight from a kettle. Bring to a gentle boil, add the pak choi leaves and cook for 60 seconds, then turn off the heat and slowly stir in the miso mixture a teaspoon at a time to prevent the almond butter from separating.

6 Divide the cooked noodles among bowls, pour over the miso broth and top with the meatballs, pak choi leaves and sliced spring onions.

FREEZER-FRIENDLY (MEATBALLS ONLY)
GLUTEN-FREE (USE GF BREADCRUMBS + NOODLES)
HIGH IN PROTEIN

THREE BEAN TORTILLA SOUP

This tortilla soup – or sopa de tortilla as it's known in Mexico – has become a family favourite in the SO VEGAN household. It's one of those humble dishes that hits the spot every time. We use a mix of black, cannellini and pinto beans – and the recipe will make more tortilla chips than you might need for your soup, but we (well, mostly our daughter Maya!) love to snack on them as a side.

EQUIPMENT: LARGE CASSEROLE POT OR LARGE SAUCEPAN / MIXING BOWL / LARGE BAKING TRAY / BAKING PAPER

SERVES **4** / PREP **8 MINS** / COOK **13 MINS**

olive oil

1 onion, peeled + finely chopped

4 garlic cloves, peeled + finely chopped

4 tortillas

salt + pepper

2 tsp ground cumin

¼ tsp cayenne pepper

4 tbsp tomato purée

3 x 400g tins of mixed beans, drained + rinsed (we use black, cannellini + pinto)

150g frozen sweetcorn

1 litre vegetable stock

1 lime, zest + juice

a large handful of fresh coriander (20g), chopped

vegan soft cheese, to serve

1 Put 1 tablespoon of olive oil into a large casserole pot or large saucepan on a medium heat. Add the onion and garlic, and cook for 6–8 minutes or until the onion is translucent.

2 Preheat the oven to 180°C fan/200°C/gas 6. Cut the tortillas in half, then slice into 3mm thin strips. Put them into a mixing bowl along with 2 teaspoons of olive oil and pinches of salt and pepper, then spread them out on a large baking tray lined with baking paper. Cook in the oven for 6–7 minutes, or until crispy and golden, giving them a stir halfway through so that they cook evenly.

3 Add the cumin, cayenne pepper and a generous pinch of salt to the pot of onion and garlic. Cook for 1 minute to toast the spices, then add the tomato purée and cook for another minute.

4 Add the beans and sweetcorn, then pour in the vegetable stock and top up with an extra 250ml of hot water. Bring to a gentle simmer and cook for 5 minutes.

5 Finally, stir in the lime zest and juice, along with most of the chopped coriander, and season to taste with more salt, if necessary.

6 Serve in bowls, with a dollop of vegan soft cheese, the rest of the chopped coriander and the tortilla chips.

FREEZER-FRIENDLY (WITHOUT TORTILLA CHIPS)

GLUTEN-FREE (USE GF TORTILLAS)

HIGH IN PROTEIN

SWEET POTATO + CHICKPEA TURMERIC CURRY

Our daughter Maya has always been fond of curry – cumin, turmeric and coriander are always a safe bet when it comes to spices. As a result, this reassuringly simple curry makes a regular appearance in our kitchen. We roast the sweet potato, which adds an extra caramelized flavour to the sweet coconut sauce.

EQUIPMENT: BAKING TRAY / BAKING PAPER / SAUCEPAN / LARGE CASSEROLE POT OR SAUCEPAN

SERVES **4** / PREP **10 MINS** / COOK **20 MINS**

600g sweet potato,
　　cut into 2cm cubes

vegetable oil

salt + pepper

280g quick-cook
　　brown rice

2 shallots, peeled +
　　finely chopped

5 garlic cloves, peeled +
　　finely chopped

2 tsp ground cumin

1 tsp ground coriander

2 tsp ground turmeric

1 x 400ml tin of
　　coconut milk

2 x 400g tins of chickpeas,
　　drained + rinsed

1 vegetable stock cube

a handful of fresh
　　coriander (15g),
　　leaves picked

1　Preheat the oven to 200°C fan/220°C/gas 7. Put the sweet potatoes on a baking tray lined with baking paper, drizzle with oil, sprinkle with pinches of salt and pepper and toss until combined, then roast for 15 minutes or until soft.

2　Meanwhile, cook the rice according to the packet instructions. Drizzle a little oil into a large casserole pot or saucepan and fry the shallots for 5 minutes. Add the garlic and spices and fry for another 2 minutes.

3　Add the coconut milk, chickpeas, crumbled stock cube, roasted sweet potato and 200ml of hot water. Bring the curry to the boil, then reduce the heat and simmer for 5 minutes. Taste and season with salt and pepper to your liking.

4　Serve the curry alongside the rice and top with fresh coriander leaves.

FREEZER-FRIENDLY (WITHOUT RICE)

GLUTEN-FREE

CHARRED SPRING ONION + EDAMAME SALAD

Charring spring onions is a really simple technique that helps to tone down their sharp flavour and it gives this warm salad a subtle smokiness. We use a griddle pan but any pan will do – and we always take the opportunity to throw them on a barbecue during the summer months.

EQUIPMENT: SAUCEPAN / GRIDDLE PAN OR FRYING PAN / SMALL BOWL

SERVES 4 / PREP 8 MINS / COOK 12 MINS

150g dry mixed quinoa

200g frozen edamame

olive oil

8 spring onions, halved
   widthways

salt + pepper

60g hazelnuts, roughly
   chopped

2 limes, juice only

4 tbsp tahini

1 tbsp maple syrup

4 handfuls of watercress

1 Put the quinoa into a saucepan and pour in water to come at least a few centimetres clear. Bring to the boil and simmer for 10 minutes. Add the edamame and boil everything for 2–3 minutes more. Once ready, drain the quinoa and edamame and set aside.

2 Meanwhile, heat a griddle pan or frying pan on a medium-high heat. Drizzle some oil across the pan, then add the spring onions, fry for 2 minutes on each side and sprinkle with a little salt and pepper. Transfer the spring onions to a plate, then add the hazelnuts to the pan and toast for 2–3 minutes, or until golden.

3 In a small bowl combine the lime juice, tahini and maple syrup to create a dressing. Add a tablespoon or 2 of water to loosen it up if needed.

4 Toss the quinoa, edamame and watercress with salt and pepper and serve warm on a large serving plate, topped with the charred spring onions, hazelnuts and the dressing.

RED BEANS + RICE

This dish has everything we absolutely adore about Southern comfort food. Simple and hearty, red beans and rice hails from New Orleans and is part of the wonderful Creole cuisine. It's traditionally stewed for hours (almost the entire day!) and served with meats. Where ours falls short on authenticity, it certainly makes up for in speed.

EQUIPMENT: LARGE CASSEROLE POT OR SAUCEPAN / SAUCEPAN

SERVES 4 / PREP 4 MINS / COOK 26 MINS

olive oil

1 onion, peeled + finely chopped

1 celery stick, finely chopped

1 red pepper, finely chopped

3 x 400g tins of kidney beans, drained + rinsed

1 bay leaf

1 tsp Tabasco sauce

500ml vegetable stock

300g basmati rice

1 tbsp miso paste (we use brown rice miso)

½ tsp mixed dried herbs

2 spring onions, sliced

1 Put 2 tablespoons of olive oil into a large casserole pot or saucepan on a medium-high heat. Add the onion, celery and red pepper, and cook for 5 minutes or until the onion is about to brown.

2 Mash a third of the beans, then add them to the pot along with the remaining whole beans, the bay leaf, Tabasco and 400ml of the vegetable stock. Bring to a strong simmer and cook for 20 minutes, stirring occasionally. If the sauce is reducing too quickly, add a splash more stock. Meanwhile, cook the rice according to the packet instructions.

3 Stir the miso paste and herbs into the beans and heat through for a minute. The sauce should be thick but runny enough that it easily falls off a spoon. Add a splash of extra water if necessary.

4 Serve the beans with the rice, topped with the spring onions.

FREEZER-FRIENDLY (WITHOUT RICE)

GLUTEN-FREE

HIGH IN PROTEIN

CRISPY CABBAGE PANCAKES

This recipe is inspired by a savoury pancake from Osaka, Japan, known as okonomiyaki. It's commonly made with egg, but instead we rely on chickpea flour (also known as gram flour), which works as a binding agent – glueing all the ingredients together to create perfectly crispy pancakes. They're super versatile, which means the toppings are up for grabs – but we find sriracha mayo and a quick homemade coleslaw always hit the spot.

EQUIPMENT: **2 MIXING BOWLS / FRYING PAN / SMALL BOWL**

SERVES **2** / PREP **10 MINS** / COOK **12 MINS**

300g white cabbage

100g red cabbage

2 carrots, sliced into matchsticks

1 lime, juice only

90g chickpea flour

2 tbsp + 1 tsp light soy sauce

3 spring onions, sliced

sesame oil

1 tbsp sriracha sauce

2 tbsp vegan mayonnaise

2 tsp maple syrup

1 First, thinly slice or grate the white and the red cabbage. To make the coleslaw, in a mixing bowl combine a third of the white cabbage with all the red cabbage, half the carrot and the lime juice. Toss through, then leave the coleslaw to one side.

2 Whisk the chickpea flour, 2 tablespoons of soy sauce and 5 tablespoons of water in a separate mixing bowl until smooth. Add the remaining white cabbage and carrot, followed by two-thirds of the spring onions. Toss the veggies into the chickpea mixture with your hands until evenly coated.

3 Drizzle some sesame oil into a frying pan on a medium heat. Transfer half the pancake mixture to the pan and press down with a spatula, easing the edges out as you go to create a large pancake roughly 1cm thick. Then pop the lid on the pan and fry for 3–5 minutes on each side until golden. Remove the pancake from the pan and cover with a clean tea towel to keep warm, then drizzle in a little more oil and repeat with the remaining mixture.

4 Meanwhile, in a small bowl combine the sriracha with the mayo and set aside.

5 Add 1 teaspoon of sesame oil, the remaining 1 teaspoon of soy sauce and the maple syrup to the coleslaw, and stir to combine.

6 To serve, top each pancake with half the coleslaw, the sriracha mayo and the rest of the spring onions.

FREEZER-FRIENDLY (PANCAKES ONLY)

GLUTEN-FREE (USE TAMARI)

PERSIAN-STYLE CHICKPEA + WALNUT STEW

This comforting stew is loosely inspired by the Persian dish fesenjan, which is traditionally made using chicken and aubergine and is served over rice. Our simplified version uses easier-to-find ingredients but – we believe – still delivers everything you want from a cosy stew, which we lightly spice with turmeric and cinnamon and serve with warm flatbreads. You can serve it over cooked rice if you prefer.

EQUIPMENT: **LARGE CASSEROLE POT OR LARGE SAUCEPAN / FOOD PROCESSOR / FRYING PAN**

SERVES **4** / PREP **6 MINS** / COOK **24 MINS**

120g walnuts

olive oil

1 red onion, peeled + finely chopped

3 garlic cloves, peeled + finely chopped

1 tsp ground cinnamon

1½ tsp ground turmeric

2 x 400g tins of chickpeas, drained + rinsed

500ml vegetable stock

1 tbsp dark soy sauce

1 lemon, juice only

salt + pepper

4 flatbreads

½ a pomegranate

1 tsp maple syrup

a handful of fresh coriander (15g), roughly chopped

1 Put the walnuts into a large casserole pot or large saucepan on a medium-high heat. Toast for 2–3 minutes, or until brown and fragrant, moving them around a few times to prevent them burning. Then transfer them to a bowl and set aside.

2 Use a clean tea towel to wipe the pot clean and remove any bits left over from the walnuts. Return the pot to a medium heat and add a generous drizzle of olive oil. Add the onion and garlic, and cook for 5 minutes or until golden brown. Stir in the cinnamon and turmeric, and cook for 1 minute.

3 Add the chickpeas to the pot, along with the vegetable stock, dark soy sauce, lemon juice and pinches of salt and pepper. Put the toasted walnuts into a food processor and blitz to a crumb, then add to the pot and give it all a good stir. Let it bubble away for 15 minutes, or until the sauce has thickened into a stew.

4 When the stew is almost ready, warm the flatbreads in a hot frying pan. Hit the skin of the pomegranate half to remove the seeds and add them to the pot (save some for topping), followed by the maple syrup. Give the stew one final stir and let it cook for a further 30 seconds or so, then serve with the warm flatbreads and top with the chopped coriander and the rest of the pomegranate seeds.

FREEZER-FRIENDLY

GLUTEN-FREE (USE GF FLATBREADS + TAMARI)

HIGH IN PROTEIN

DOUBLE BEAN STROGANOFF

It's hard to think of a meal we love more – and cook more often – than stroganoff. Whatever variation of this classic Russian dish we choose to make, it just never disappoints. Here we turn to cannellini and fine green beans, which offer a more subtle flavour than the traditional mushrooms but work seamlessly with the slightly sour and creamy sauce. Try to avoid using a vegan cream that is too sweet – we find oat-based creams work best.

EQUIPMENT: **LARGE FRYING PAN / SAUCEPAN**

SERVES **4** / PREP **8 MINS** / COOK **15 MINS**

olive oil

1 onion, peeled + finely
    chopped

300g jasmine rice

3 garlic cloves, peeled +
    finely chopped

1 tsp smoked paprika

1 vegetable stock cube

150g fine green beans,
    ends trimmed

2 x 400g tins of cannellini
    beans, drained + rinsed

200ml vegan cream (we
    use oat)

2 tsp apple cider vinegar

salt + pepper

a large handful of fresh
    parsley (20g), roughly
    chopped

1 Drizzle a generous amount of olive oil into a large frying pan on a medium heat. Add the onion and cook for 8 minutes, or until brown. Meanwhile, cook the rice according to the packet instructions.

2 Stir the garlic and smoked paprika into the pan and cook for a minute. Then dissolve the stock cube in a jug with 150ml of hot water straight from a kettle, and pour into the pan. Throw in the green beans and cook for 3–4 minutes, or until the beans are tender but still crunchy.

3 Mash a quarter of the cannellini beans using a fork or a potato masher, then add them to the pan along with the remaining whole cannellini beans, the cream, vinegar, a pinch of salt and a generous pinch of pepper. Cook for another minute or two to bring all the flavours together, then stir in most of the chopped parsley and season to taste with extra salt and pepper, if necessary.

4 Serve the stroganoff over the rice and top with the rest of the chopped parsley.

FREEZER-FRIENDLY (WITHOUT RICE)

GLUTEN-FREE

BARBECUED MUSHROOM TACOS

We've always been big fans of Cajun seasoning, which gives these meaty mushrooms a slightly spicy kick. But you can use whichever seasoning mix you prefer – fajita, barbecue or regular all-purpose seasoning would also work really well. This recipe makes 6 tacos, which will serve 2 people well – especially with some tortilla chips on the side.

EQUIPMENT: **BAKING TRAY / BAKING PAPER / 2 MIXING BOWLS / FRYING PAN**

SERVES **2** / PREP **5 MINS** / COOK **20 MINS**

1 tbsp Cajun seasoning

olive oil

4 portobello mushrooms

3 tbsp barbecue sauce

1 mango

a bunch of fresh coriander (30g), large stalks removed

½ a red chilli, sliced

1 lime, juice only

6 small tortillas

tortilla chips, to serve

1 Preheat the oven to 200°C fan/220°C/gas 7 and line a baking tray with baking paper. Combine the Cajun seasoning with 2 tablespoons of olive oil in a mixing bowl, then brush the mixture evenly over the mushrooms, including all over the gills. Drizzle some more olive oil into a frying pan on a medium heat, then add the mushrooms to the pan, gills facing down. Cook for 4–6 minutes on each side, or until charred, pushing down on the mushrooms using a potato masher or metal spatula while they cook, to extract more moisture (don't worry if they break apart a little).

2 Transfer the mushrooms to a chopping board. Slice them ½cm thick, then transfer them to the mixing bowl you used earlier. Stir the barbecue sauce into the mushrooms, then lay them out evenly on the baking tray. Cook in the oven for 10–15 minutes.

3 Meanwhile, trim the mango around the stone so you end up with 2 halves, then criss-cross the flesh of each half and scoop out the cubed mango. Trim any flesh from around the stone, then slice the mango into small pieces and put it all into a second mixing bowl. Roughly chop a third of the coriander, then add it to the mixing bowl along with the chilli and lime juice. Give it a good stir, then set aside.

4 Wipe clean the pan you used earlier and use it to warm the tortillas on a high heat, then build your tacos using the warm tortillas, barbecued mushrooms, mango salsa, some crushed tortilla chips and leftover coriander leaves, and eat them alongside some extra tortilla chips.

GLUTEN-FREE (USE GF BBQ SAUCE, TORTILLAS + CHIPS)

LEMON TOFU + NOODLES

You've probably spotted lemon chicken on menus in Chinese restaurants here in the UK, but you'll have a hard time finding it in China. Despite its confusing origins, in our minds there's still a lot to like about this takeout classic. For our recipe, crispy tofu chunks take pride of place in a sweet and sour sauce, which we throw together with noodles and peppers.

EQUIPMENT: 2 MIXING BOWLS / WOK OR LARGE NON-STICK FRYING PAN / SAUCEPAN

SERVES 2 / PREP 10 MINS / COOK 12 MINS

300g block of extra
  firm tofu, drained

1 tbsp + 2 tsp cornflour

salt + pepper

vegetable oil

1½ lemons

1½ tbsp caster sugar

1 tbsp light soy sauce

160g wheat noodles

½ a red pepper, cut into
  squares

½ a green pepper, cut into
  squares

3 garlic cloves, peeled +
  sliced

½ a thumb of fresh ginger
  (15g), peeled + sliced

1 Tear the tofu into bite-size pieces and combine it in a mixing bowl with 1 tablespoon of cornflour and pinches of salt and pepper. Put a generous splash of oil into a wok or large non-stick frying pan on a medium-high heat. Add the tofu and fry for 8–10 minutes, or until it's golden and crispy all over, then transfer to a plate and wipe out the wok.

2 Meanwhile, finely grate 1 lemon until you have 1 teaspoon of zest. Combine the zest in a mixing bowl with the juice from 1 lemon, the caster sugar, soy sauce, the remaining 2 teaspoons of cornflour, a small pinch of salt and 100ml of water, then set aside.

3 Cook the noodles according to the packet instructions, then drain and set aside.

4 Return the wok to a medium-high heat and add a small splash of oil. Add the red and green pepper, garlic and ginger, stir-fry for 2 minutes, then lower the heat and stir in the sauce. Cook for 1–2 minutes to thicken the sauce slightly, then stir in the crispy tofu and the cooked noodles and serve. Finally, slice the remaining lemon half and use to garnish.

GLUTEN-FREE (USE GF NOODLES + TAMARI)

HIGH IN PROTEIN

MARMITE PIE

Pots of Marmite don't last very long in our house. If it's not being smeared all over toast, it's usually being added to stews and pies to give depth and much-needed savouriness, which you'd otherwise get from adding meat. This 30-minute wonder pie is as simple as they come, with familiar flavours and easy-to-find ingredients, which is the reason we love it so much.

EQUIPMENT: **LARGE CASSEROLE POT OR LARGE SAUCEPAN / BAKING DISH**

SERVES **6** / PREP **6 MINS** / COOK **24 MINS**

3 tbsp vegan butter or
   margarine

1 onion, peeled + finely
   chopped

3 carrots, diced

1 vegetable stock cube

3 x 400g tins of green
   lentils, drained + rinsed

200g frozen peas

2 tbsp plain flour

2 tbsp Marmite

2 tbsp tomato purée

3 sprigs of fresh rosemary,
   leaves picked + roughly
   chopped

1 tbsp wholegrain mustard

1 tbsp balsamic vinegar

salt + pepper

1 x 320g sheet of vegan
   puff pastry

1 Preheat the oven to 200°C fan/220°C/gas 7. Put 2 tablespoons of the butter into a large casserole pot or large saucepan on a medium-high heat. Add the onion and carrot and cook for 6 minutes, or until the onion is brown.

2 Dissolve the vegetable stock cube in a jug with 350ml of hot water straight from a kettle and pour into the pot. Add the lentils, peas, flour, Marmite, tomato purée, rosemary, mustard, vinegar, a small pinch of salt and a big pinch of pepper. Stir well to make sure the Marmite is distributed evenly in the mixture, then pour it into a baking dish approx. 25cm x 30cm.

3 Unroll the puff pastry sheet and use it to cover the dish, slicing off any pastry hanging over the edge. Fold the edges of the pastry in on themselves, then make a few cuts to allow the steam to escape. Quickly melt the remaining tablespoon of butter, brush it all over the pastry top, and bake the pie for 15–25 minutes, or until the pastry is cooked and is a lovely golden brown (this might take a little longer depending on your oven).

GLUTEN-FREE (USE GF PASTRY + FLOUR
+ SWAP MARMITE FOR TAMARI)

ONION PAKORAS
WITH LIME SALSA

Pakoras are typically served with a chutney or raita, but lately we've been pairing these crispy Indian fritters with a gorgeous lime, coriander and tomato salsa, which brings a big burst of freshness and means they can double up as a snack or a lunch.

EQUIPMENT: **2 MIXING BOWLS / 2 LARGE FRYING PANS**

MAKES **20 PAKORAS** / PREP **10 MINS** / COOK **18 MINS**

200g chickpea flour

1 tbsp garam masala

1 tsp ground turmeric

salt + pepper

4 large onions (650g), finely sliced

100g baby spinach

vegetable oil

a handful of fresh coriander (15g), roughly chopped, stalks + all

450g cherry tomatoes, quartered

½ a green chilli, seeds removed, finely chopped

1 lime, juice only

1 Put the chickpea flour, garam masala, turmeric and generous pinches of salt and pepper into a mixing bowl, along with 180ml of cold water. Whisk until combined, to create a thick smooth batter, then add the onions and spinach and mix until evenly coated. Add a small splash of extra water if necessary to make sure the onion and spinach are fully coated in the batter.

2 Heat two large frying pans on a medium-high heat and drizzle generously with oil. To make each pakora, add 2 tablespoons of the mixture to the frying pan and push down with a spatula to flatten it out. Repeat until no more pakoras fit into the pans, then cover with a lid and fry for 2–3 minutes on each side until golden. Repeat until all the pakora mixture has been used up, adding a glug more oil to the pan each time. Transfer the pakoras to a plate lined with kitchen paper as you go, and sprinkle them with salt.

3 Meanwhile, prepare the salsa by combining the coriander in a second mixing bowl with the cherry tomatoes, chilli, lime juice and pinches of salt and pepper. Toss to combine, then spoon all over the pakoras to serve.

FREEZER-FRIENDLY (PAKORAS ONLY)

GLUTEN-FREE

CAJUN BREADED CAULIFLOWER SALAD

Cajun seasoning is one of our favourite spice blends and we put it to good use here. It's smoky, peppery and earthy, which adds depth to this crunchy cauliflower salad. We prefer to use an oat-based Greek style yoghurt, which we find is less sweet and better complements the dish. Serve as a lunch or alongside a cooked grain – such as quinoa or brown rice – for dinner.

EQUIPMENT: **LARGE BAKING TRAY / BAKING PAPER / 2 MIXING BOWLS**

SERVES **3–4** / PREP **15 MINS** / COOK **15 MINS**

100g plain flour

120ml plant-based milk, plus extra

salt

1 tbsp + ½ tsp Cajun seasoning

120g panko breadcrumbs

olive oil

1 medium cauliflower, cut into small florets

100g lamb's lettuce

150g cherry tomatoes, halved

½ a red onion, peeled + finely sliced

130g vegan yoghurt (we use oat Greek style)

½ a lime, juice only

1 Preheat the oven to 220°C fan/240°C/gas 9 and line a large baking tray with baking paper.

2 Combine the flour, plant-based milk, a pinch of salt and 1 teaspoon of Cajun seasoning in a mixing bowl. Add a splash more milk if the batter seems too thick, then set aside.

3 Put the breadcrumbs, 2 teaspoons of Cajun seasoning and 1 tablespoon of olive oil into a separate mixing bowl. Use your fingers to combine the ingredients, then set aside.

4 Add all the cauliflower to the batter and stir until the florets are fully coated. Then, one floret at a time, cover the cauliflower all over with the breadcrumbs and place the florets on the baking tray. Bake for 15 minutes, or until cooked through but still crunchy.

5 Meanwhile, rinse out and dry the two bowls you used earlier. Put the lettuce, tomatoes, red onion, 1 teaspoon of olive oil and a small pinch of salt into the large bowl, then mix and set aside. In the other bowl combine the yoghurt with the remaining ½ teaspoon of Cajun seasoning and the lime juice. Add a splash of plant-based milk to loosen the dressing, then set aside.

6 When the cauliflower is ready, put the salad on a large serving plate, top with the cauliflower, then drizzle over some of the dressing and serve the rest alongside.

GLUTEN-FREE (USE GF FLOUR + BREADCRUMBS)

ONE-TRAY

ZA'ATAR VEGGIE FLATBREADS

One of our favourite places to immerse ourselves in food culture is Brockley Market – just a few miles down the road from us in south-east London. You'll find lots of independent stalls and street food traders, such as Mike + Ollie, who serve homemade flatbreads, including a delicious vegan version using squash. The not-so-secret ingredient in their repertoire is za'atar, which they smother all over the flatbreads – and it's the inspiration behind this colourful and flavoursome recipe.

EQUIPMENT: LARGE BAKING TRAY / BAKING PAPER / 2 SMALL BOWLS

SERVES **4** / PREP **8 MINS** / COOK **18 MINS**

1 courgette, sliced into
   rings
½ a cauliflower, cut into
   small florets
1 red onion, peeled +
   roughly sliced
1 x 400g tin of chickpeas,
   drained + rinsed
4 garlic cloves, unpeeled
olive oil
salt + pepper
1 tbsp sumac
4 flatbreads
2 tbsp za'atar
4 tbsp vegan mayonnaise
2 tomatoes, diced
a handful of fresh
   coriander (15g),
   leaves picked

1 Preheat the oven to 200°C fan/220°C/gas 7 and line a large baking tray with baking paper.

2 Put the courgette, cauliflower, red onion, chickpeas and garlic on the tray. Drizzle with oil and sprinkle generously with salt, pepper and the sumac. Toss to combine and roast for 15 minutes, then lay the flatbreads on top of the veggies and roast everything for another 3–5 minutes, or until the flatbreads are warmed through.

3 Meanwhile, in a small bowl combine the za'atar with 3 tablespoons of oil. Remove the tray from the oven and spread the za'atar oil over the flatbreads, then place them on serving plates.

4 Once the garlic is cool enough to touch, remove the skins. Mash the flesh with a fork, then transfer it to a small bowl along with the mayonnaise and 1 tablespoon of water, and stir to combine.

5 Top the flatbreads with the roasted veggies, tomatoes, a drizzle of the garlic mayonnaise and a sprinkling of coriander leaves.

GLUTEN-FREE (USE GF FLATBREADS)

CRISPY CHILLI TOFU SALAD

This dish is inspired by the Chinese takeaway chilli beef, and we serve our tofu with a tangy salad for a lighter touch. Extra firm tofu shouldn't require pressing, so it's a great time-saver for recipes like this. But if your tofu is a little soft, be sure to press it beforehand.

EQUIPMENT: NON-STICK FRYING PAN OR WOK / SMALL BOWL / LARGE MIXING BOWL

SERVES 2 / PREP 10 MINS / COOK 10 MINS

400g block of
    extra firm tofu,
    drained
salt + pepper
2 tbsp cornflour
sesame oil
3 tbsp ketchup
1 tbsp dark soy sauce
1½ tbsp caster sugar
1 lime
3 garlic cloves, peeled
    + finely chopped
½ a thumb of fresh
    ginger (15g), peeled
    + finely chopped
1 red chilli, half
    chopped + half
    sliced
½ a romaine lettuce,
    leaves sliced
2 spring onions,
    thinly sliced

a handful of fresh
    coriander (15g),
    leaves picked
a handful of salted
    peanuts

FOR THE DRESSING

½ tsp dark soy sauce
½ tsp sesame oil
1 lime, juice only
1 tsp caster sugar

1 Using your fingers, break up the tofu into 2cm bite-size pieces and put them on a plate. Sprinkle with salt, pepper and the cornflour and toss until fully combined.

2 Pour a generous splash of sesame oil into a non-stick frying pan or wok on a medium-high heat and fry the tofu for 8–10 minutes, or until golden and crispy on all sides.

3 Meanwhile, in a small bowl combine the ketchup, soy sauce, sugar, the zest of half the lime and the juice of the whole lime. Stir to combine and leave to one side.

4 Add the garlic, ginger and the chopped half of the chilli to the tofu pan and fry for 1 minute. Stir in the ketchup sauce for 30 seconds or so, until the tofu is fully coated, then remove the pan from the heat.

5 Put the sliced chilli, lettuce, spring onions, coriander and peanuts into a large mixing bowl (leave a few peanuts to one side to decorate with later).

6 Rinse out the small bowl from earlier, add the dressing ingredients, stir, and pour over the salad. Toss to combine, then top the salad with the tofu and finish with a sprinkling of peanuts.

GLUTEN-FREE (USE TAMARI)
HIGH IN PROTEIN
ONE-PAN

PEKING 'DUCK' RICE BOWL

Ever since we turned vegan, jackfruit has remained one of our favourite substitutes for meat, thanks to its stringy texture and its habit of soaking up whatever flavour we throw at it. Here we 'unroll' the classic Chinese dish Peking duck pancakes by ditching the pancakes and serving our jackfruit in a bowl with fluffy rice. If you prefer, you can swap the jackfruit for around 500g of sliced shiitake mushrooms, which will cook in the same amount of time.

EQUIPMENT: **BAKING TRAY / BAKING PAPER / 2 SMALL BOWLS / SAUCEPAN**

SERVES **4** / PREP **10 MINS** / COOK **20 MINS**

½ a red onion, peeled + thinly sliced

2 tsp apple cider vinegar

2 x 400g tins of jackfruit in water

sesame oil

280g jasmine rice

1 tsp Chinese five-spice

4 tbsp hoisin sauce

1 tbsp light soy sauce

1 cucumber, diced

2 spring onions, sliced

plum sauce, to serve

1 Preheat the oven to 220°C fan/240°C/gas 9 and line a baking tray with baking paper. Combine the red onion and apple cider vinegar in a small bowl, then set aside to pickle.

2 Drain and rinse the jackfruit, then pat dry. Slice off the hard cores and thinly slice them into strips, then use your fingers to tear apart the remaining stringy flesh. Add all the jackfruit to the baking tray and drizzle over some sesame oil. Stir to combine, then roast in the oven for 15 minutes, stirring halfway through.

3 Meanwhile, cook the rice according to the packet instructions, then cover and set aside. Combine the Chinese five-spice, hoisin sauce and soy sauce in a small bowl. Once the jackfruit has finished cooking, remove it from the oven and stir in the sauce, then roast again for another 5–10 minutes, or until it's crispy around the edges.

4 Serve the jackfruit in a bowl, along with the rice, cucumber, spring onions, pickled red onion and a dollop of plum sauce.

AUBERGINE RAGOUT
WITH NEW POTATOES

Ragout is typically stewed for hours over a low heat, but that's a luxury we can rarely afford when our evenings also involve getting the kids fed and in bed on time. Instead we grill aubergine until it's soft in the middle, then pull out the smoky flesh and add it to a rich tomato sauce. If you don't want to use fresh tomatoes, you can swap in two tins of chopped tomatoes instead.

EQUIPMENT: BAKING TRAY / LARGE SAUCEPAN / CASSEROLE POT OR SAUCEPAN

SERVES **3–4** / PREP **12 MINS** / COOK **17 MINS**

2 aubergines

800g new potatoes

olive oil

1 onion, peeled + finely chopped

4 garlic cloves, peeled + finely chopped

600g ripe tomatoes, chopped

1½ tsp dried oregano

1½ tbsp dark soy sauce

2 tsp balsamic vinegar

salt + pepper

1 Prick each aubergine half a dozen times with a fork, then place them on a baking tray and cook under a grill on high for 15–20 minutes, or until soft in the middle, turning halfway through. When cool enough, cut the aubergines in half horizontally and use a fork to pull out the flesh.

2 Meanwhile, put the potatoes into a large saucepan, cover with cold water, add a pinch of salt, bring to the boil and cook for 10–15 minutes or until tender, then drain and set aside.

3 While the aubergine and potatoes are cooking, drizzle a splash of olive oil into a casserole pot or saucepan on a medium heat. Add the onion and garlic, and cook for 8 minutes or until brown. Stir in the tomatoes, oregano, soy sauce and balsamic vinegar, then cook for 8–10 minutes, or until the tomatoes have broken down into a thick sauce. Finally stir in the pulled aubergine, season to taste with salt and pepper, and cook for another minute. You can add a splash of water if necessary to help loosen the sauce a little.

4 To serve, crush the potatoes with a fork, put them on a plate with the aubergine ragout, drizzle over a splash of extra olive oil and sprinkle over some freshly ground black pepper.

FREEZER-FRIENDLY (RAGOUT ONLY)

GLUTEN-FREE (USE TAMARI)

MUSTARD-CRUSTED CAULIFLOWER STEAKS

Our diet growing up was mostly based on a simple principle: meat and two veg. Things have moved on a lot from then, but the truth is part of us still misses the simplicity of roasting something and serving it alongside veggies. So step forward our cauliflower steaks, which we roast with a panko and mustard crumb and serve with potatoes and wilted spinach. Simple food at its best!

EQUIPMENT: LARGE BAKING TRAY / BAKING PAPER / LARGE SAUCEPAN / 2 SMALL BOWLS / LARGE FRYING PAN

SERVES 2 / PREP 7 MINS / COOK 20 MINS

1 cauliflower

olive oil

salt + pepper

400g new potatoes

1 tbsp wholegrain mustard

4 tbsp panko breadcrumbs

300g baby spinach

a small handful of fresh dill (10g), chopped

100g vegan yoghurt (we use oat Greek style)

½ a lemon, sliced into wedges

1 Preheat the oven to 200°C fan/220°C/gas 7 and line a large baking tray with baking paper. Remove the leaves from the cauliflower and slice the head down the middle. Cut a 2cm thick steak from each half of the head so you have two steaks (save the rest for another time), then transfer the steaks to the baking tray. Drizzle both sides with olive oil and season with salt and pepper, then bake for 10 minutes.

2 Meanwhile, put the potatoes into a large saucepan and cover with cold water. Add a pinch of salt, bring to the boil and cook for 10–15 minutes or until tender, then drain and set aside.

3 In a small bowl combine the mustard with the breadcrumbs, 1 tablespoon of olive oil and small pinches of salt and pepper. Remove the cauliflower from the oven, flip over the steaks and spoon the crumb mixture over the top of each steak, then return them to the oven for another 10 minutes.

4 Put the spinach into a large frying pan and cook over a low heat until it has wilted. Combine the dill and yoghurt in a small bowl. To serve, put the cauliflower steaks on plates alongside the potatoes, spinach, yoghurt and lemon wedges.

COCA DE TOMATE

The more we explore Spanish cuisine, the more we fall in love with its simple and uncomplicated use of fresh ingredients. Coca is a type of Spanish flatbread, which usually comes with a few choice toppings. For this dish we use fresh ripe tomatoes – usually the plum variety (if we can get our hands on them), which have a higher ratio of flesh to pulp – on top of our tried-and-tested 'instant' dough for an easy meal or snack.

EQUIPMENT: **LARGE BAKING TRAY / BAKING PAPER / MIXING BOWL / SMALL BOWL**

SERVES **4** / PREP **10 MINS** / COOK **12 MINS**

280g self-raising flour, plus extra

200g vegan yoghurt (we use oat or unsweetened soy)

salt + pepper

olive oil

3 garlic cloves, peeled + grated

400g ripe tomatoes, sliced 3mm thick

1½ tbsp pine nuts

a small handful of fresh basil (10g), chopped

1 Preheat the oven to 200°C fan/220°C/gas 7 and line a large baking tray with baking paper.

2 Using a spoon, combine the flour, yoghurt and generous pinches of salt and pepper in a mixing bowl. Then tip the dough out on to a worktop and knead for a minute. Dust a clean worktop with flour, then roll the dough out into a rectangle roughly 2–3mm thick and approximately 30cm x 25cm in size.

3 Transfer the dough to the lined baking tray. Drizzle a splash of olive oil on top of the dough and brush it all over the surface. Sprinkle over the garlic, then place the sliced tomatoes on top, overlapping if necessary and leaving a 1cm border around the edges for the crust. Sprinkle over the pine nuts, followed by pinches of salt and pepper, and drizzle over another splash of olive oil. Bake for 12–15 minutes, or until the crust is golden brown.

4 Meanwhile, combine the basil with 2 tablespoons of olive oil in a small bowl. When the bread is ready, spoon the basil oil over the top and slice to serve.

CUMIN ROASTED CAULIFLOWER
WITH COUSCOUS + RED PEPPER SAUCE

Ever since we first tried muhammara (a wonderful Middle Eastern red pepper dip), we've been obsessed with whipping up new adaptations of it in our day-to-day meals. Here we use a simplified version, which we drizzle over cumin roasted cauliflower and couscous. Yum.

EQUIPMENT: LARGE ROASTING TRAY / LARGE MIXING BOWL / FOOD PROCESSOR

SERVES **3–4** / PREP **10 MINS** / COOK **20 MINS**

1 cauliflower

1½ tsp cumin seeds

salt + pepper

olive oil

250g couscous

400ml vegetable stock

160g jarred roasted red
   peppers, rinsed

a bunch of fresh parsley
   (30g), leaves picked,
   stalks reserved

40g walnuts

1 lemon

1 Preheat the oven to 200°C fan/220°C/gas 7. Tear the leaves off the cauliflower, rinse them and leave to one side. Break up the cauliflower into florets. Put the florets into a large roasting tray with the cumin seeds, pinches of salt and pepper and a splash of olive oil. Mix, then roast for 10 minutes.

2 Put the couscous into a large mixing bowl, stir in 350ml of the vegetable stock, then cover and leave to one side.

3 Put the red peppers and parsley stalks into a food processor with the walnuts, 3 tablespoons of olive oil, the juice from half the lemon and small pinches of salt and pepper. Blitz until smooth.

4 Remove the tray from the oven. Push the florets to one side and add the cauliflower leaves. Season with small pinches of salt and pepper, drizzle with olive oil, mix, then roast for 10 minutes, or until the florets are tender and the leaves are crispy.

5 Roughly chop the parsley leaves. When you're almost ready to serve, stir about two-thirds of the chopped parsley and the remaining 50ml of vegetable stock into the couscous.

6 To serve, place the couscous on a large serving plate, top with the cauliflower florets and leaves (along with all the cumin seeds from the tray), drizzle over the red pepper sauce and sprinkle over the rest of the parsley leaves. Serve any leftover sauce in a bowl alongside.

7 Finally, slice the remaining lemon half into wedges to serve. Delicious!

HARISSA + WALNUT STUFFED COURGETTES

These fiery stuffed courgettes are delicious on their own or, as we sometimes serve them, alongside a leafy salad. Rose harissa paste is more subtle than regular harissa paste and gives this dish its characteristic sweet and smoky flavour.

EQUIPMENT: **FRYING PAN** / **ROASTING TRAY**

SERVES **4** / PREP **7 MINS** / COOK **23 MINS**

4 courgettes

olive oil

1 red onion, peeled + diced

130g walnuts, finely
   chopped

2 tbsp rose harissa paste

80g black olives, sliced,
   plus 1 tbsp brine from
   the jar

salt + pepper

1 sprig of fresh thyme,
   leaves picked

½ a lemon, zest only

1 Preheat the oven to 220°C fan/240°C/gas 9.

2 Cut the courgettes in half lengthways and use a teaspoon to scoop out the flesh from the middle, leaving the edges clear. Roughly chop the scooped-out flesh and leave to one side.

3 Heat a little oil in a frying pan on a medium heat. Add the onion and fry for 5 minutes. Then add 100g of the walnuts, the rose harissa paste, the olives along with 1 tablespoon of their brine, and the courgette flesh. Generously sprinkle with salt and pepper, then fry for 3 minutes, or until heated through and combined.

4 Place the courgette halves on a large roasting tray, leaving space between them, then drizzle with a little oil and spoon the walnut mixture into the middle of each courgette. Bake for 15–20 minutes.

5 Meanwhile, wipe out the pan that had the walnut mixture in it and add the remaining walnuts, along with generous pinches of salt and pepper and the thyme leaves. Toast on a medium-high heat for 3–5 minutes, then toss in the grated lemon zest and leave to one side.

6 When the courgettes are ready, sprinkle over the walnut crumb and serve.

FREEZER-FRIENDLY
GLUTEN-FREE

CHILLI BROCCOLI
WITH SWEET POTATO MASH

This vibrant dish uses really easy-to-find ingredients to deliver totally winning flavour combinations. Our cumin-spiced sweet potato mash is the base, which we top with crunchy broccoli florets and a herby tahini dressing. Delish!

EQUIPMENT: SAUCEPAN / SMALL BOWL / WOK OR LARGE FRYING PAN

SERVES 4 / PREP 10 MINS / COOK 10 MINS

1kg sweet potato, peeled + cubed

½ tsp ground cumin

olive oil

salt + pepper

5 tbsp tahini

a handful of fresh parsley (15g), roughly chopped

½ a lemon, juice only

2 broccoli, cut into small florets

¼ tsp chilli flakes

2 garlic cloves, peeled + sliced

1 Put the sweet potatoes into a saucepan and cover with boiling water. Boil for 10 minutes, or until soft, then drain and leave to steam dry for 2 minutes. Put the sweet potatoes back into the saucepan and mash until smooth, then stir in the cumin, 2 tablespoons of olive oil and small pinches of salt and pepper.

2 Meanwhile, combine the tahini, parsley, lemon juice, 4 tablespoons of water and small pinches of salt and pepper in a small bowl. If the dressing is too thick, add a splash more water, then set aside.

3 Next, drizzle a splash of olive oil into a wok or large frying pan on a medium heat. Add the broccoli florets and fry for 2–3 minutes, or until tender and brown around the edges. Add the chilli flakes and garlic, cook for 30 seconds, then remove from the heat.

4 To serve, divide the sweet potato mash among four plates, top with the chilli broccoli and drizzle over the parsley tahini.

SRIRACHA ROASTED CAULIFLOWER BOWL

This bowl is a snapshot of how we love to cook quick and easy midweek meals. Spicy, roasted cauliflower, a grain (here we use bulgur wheat), fresh veggies and a delicious dressing. It's a tried-and-tested approach that works in various forms – you can sub cauliflower with broccoli, bulgur with rice, and throw together whatever salad or dressing you fancy.

EQUIPMENT: BAKING TRAY / BAKING PAPER / LARGE MIXING BOWL / SAUCEPAN / SMALL BOWL

SERVES **3–4** / PREP **10 MINS** / COOK **15 MINS**

2 tbsp sriracha sauce, plus extra

3 tbsp maple syrup

1 tbsp vegetable oil

1½ tbsp light soy sauce

1 large cauliflower, cut into florets

200g bulgur wheat

3 tbsp tahini

½ a cucumber, thinly sliced

200g radishes, thinly sliced

2 tsp sesame seeds

1 Preheat the oven to 200°C fan/220°C/gas 7 and line a baking tray with baking paper. In a large mixing bowl combine the sriracha with 2 tablespoons of maple syrup, the oil and 1 tablespoon of soy sauce. Add the cauliflower florets to the bowl and toss to combine, then place them on the baking tray. Roast for 15–20 minutes, until the cauliflower has some bite left to it and is slightly charred.

2 Meanwhile, cook the bulgur wheat according to the packet instructions. For the dressing, in a small bowl combine the tahini with ½ tablespoon of soy sauce and 1 tablespoon of maple syrup, adding 1 tablespoon of water at a time until smooth.

3 Divide the bulgur among bowls, top with the cauliflower, and finish with cucumber, radishes, a drizzle of tahini dressing, some more sriracha and a sprinkling of sesame seeds.

GLUTEN-FREE (USE RICE + TAMARI)

30 MINS OR MORE

SMASHED NEW POTATO SALAD
WITH GARLIC DRESSING

Smashed potatoes are back in vogue and we're all for it. Crushing the spuds helps the oil soak into the skin – giving you crispy potatoes with minimal fuss – and in our opinion you can't beat pairing them with our garlic and yoghurt dressing. Heaven.

EQUIPMENT: LARGE BAKING TRAY / FOIL OR BAKING PAPER / MIXING BOWL / SMALL BOWL

SERVES **4** / PREP **10 MINS** / COOK **50 MINS**

1kg new potatoes

olive oil

salt + pepper

1 bulb of garlic, plus 1 garlic clove

180g green beans, ends trimmed

2 gem lettuces, cut into quarters

250ml vegan yoghurt (we use oat Greek style)

1 lemon

50g pitted green olives, sliced into rings

a large bunch of fresh dill, leaves roughly torn

1 Preheat the oven to 200°C fan/220°C/gas 7. Put the potatoes into a large baking tray, drizzle them with olive oil and sprinkle with salt and pepper. Toss, then roast for 30 minutes.

2 Meanwhile, remove the papery skin from the bulb of garlic and cut 1cm off the top of the bulb. Drizzle the exposed cloves with olive oil, then wrap the bulb in foil or baking paper and set aside. Remove the tray from the oven and smash the potatoes with a masher or fork. Add the garlic bulb to the tray and roast everything for another 10 minutes.

3 Put the green beans and gem lettuce into a mixing bowl, drizzle with olive oil and season with salt and pepper. Toss, then pick out the green beans, add them to the roasting tray with the other veggies, and roast for 5 minutes.

4 Finally, add the gem lettuce to the tray and roast everything for a final 5–8 minutes, until the lettuce is charred and the green beans are soft.

5 Once the garlic bulb is cool enough to touch, squeeze the garlic out of the cloves and chop it up. Put it into a small bowl with the yoghurt, the juice from half the lemon and pinches of salt and pepper. Peel and dice the remaining raw garlic clove and add it to the bowl, then stir.

6 To finish, squeeze the juice from the remaining half lemon all over the traybake, sprinkle the olives evenly over the top, and spoon over the yoghurt dressing. Scatter over the fresh dill and finally drizzle with olive oil.

GLUTEN-FREE
ONE-TRAY

MUSHROOM + DATE PIE

Forget about chopping your mushrooms. Cooking them whole is a great way to preserve their tender texture and earthy flavour, which we combine with sweet dates in this seriously comforting pie. If you want to avoid red wine, you can switch it for 1 tablespoon of balsamic vinegar (add it after cooking the flour).

EQUIPMENT: LARGE CASSEROLE POT OR LARGE SAUCEPAN / PIE DISH

SERVES 4 / PREP 10 MINS / COOK 1 HR 2 MINS

olive oil

2 onions, peeled + sliced
   into wedges

500g chestnut mushrooms

4 garlic cloves, peeled +
   finely chopped

1 sprig of fresh rosemary,
   leaves picked +
   chopped

3 bay leaves

125ml vegan red wine

2 tbsp plain flour

250g carrots, sliced into
   1cm rings

250ml vegetable stock

2 dates, pitted + chopped

salt + pepper

4 large potatoes

1 Pour a generous glug of olive oil into a large casserole pot or large saucepan on a medium heat. Add the onion wedges and fry for 4 minutes, then add the whole mushrooms and fry for 10 minutes.

2 Preheat the oven to 180°C fan/200°C/gas 6.

3 Add the garlic, rosemary and bay leaves to the pot and fry for 1 minute. Then pour in the wine and simmer for 4 minutes.

4 Stir in the flour and cook for 30 seconds. Add the carrots, stock and dates, along with pinches of salt and pepper, and simmer for 2 minutes.

5 Transfer the mushroom filling to a pie dish. Slice the potatoes into ½cm thick slices and lay them on top of the filling, overlapping the slices as you go. Finish with a drizzle of olive oil and sprinkle with more salt and pepper. Roast for 40 minutes, or until the potatoes are tender and golden brown.

FREEZER-FRIENDLY

GLUTEN-FREE (USE GF FLOUR)

GNOCCHI ALL'AMATRICIANA

Amatriciana is a pasta sauce that originates from the town of Amatrice in central Italy. You'll find it served all over the region and in Roman trattorias. It's usually made with pork, but we turn to our trusty mushrooms, cooking them with soy sauce and smoked paprika to add depth and a smoky flavour, then combining them with a rich tomato sauce and fluffy gnocchi.

EQUIPMENT: **FRYING PAN / SAUCEPAN**

SERVES **4** / PREP **10 MINS** / COOK **27 MINS**

olive oil

300g closed-cup mushrooms, roughly chopped

1 tsp smoked paprika

2 tbsp dark soy sauce

1 onion, peeled + finely chopped

3 garlic cloves, peeled + finely chopped

½ tsp chilli flakes

1 x 400g tin of chopped tomatoes

600g vegan gnocchi

80g vegan Parmesan, grated

1 Heat a drizzle of oil in a frying pan on a medium-high heat. Add the mushrooms and fry for 8 minutes. Then add the smoked paprika and soy sauce and fry for 2 minutes. Transfer the mushrooms to a plate and save for later.

2 Add another drizzle of oil to the pan and fry the onion, garlic and chilli flakes for 2 minutes on a medium-high heat. Add the tomatoes and simmer on a low heat for 15 minutes.

3 When the sauce has 5 minutes' cooking time left, cook the gnocchi according to the packet instructions. Once they have floated to the surface, spoon them into the tomato sauce along with a generous splash of the cooking water, a touch more oil, most of the grated Parmesan (save some to serve with) and the reserved mushrooms. Stir until everything is completely combined and the sauce is glossy.

4 Serve with an extra sprinkling of grated Parmesan.

GLUTEN-FREE (USE GF GNOCCHI + TAMARI)

FAMILY PASTA TRAYBAKE

Our criteria for cooking midweek family meals is simple: create as little mess as possible – and that's exactly where this simple one-tray pasta bake steps in. Use up whatever pasta is hiding at the back of the cupboard – combinations of penne, macaroni and fusilli will all work wonders. If you can't find olive tapenade, vegan pesto will also work fine – and you can store leftovers in the freezer for a few months.

EQUIPMENT: **DEEP ROASTING DISH / LARGE BAKING TRAY OR FOIL**

SERVES **4** / PREP **15 MINS** / COOK **45 MINS**

400g pasta (we use
    rigatoni)

50g vegan Parmesan,
    grated, plus extra

1 courgette, diced

2 red peppers, diced

2 x 400g tins of chopped
    tomatoes

3 tbsp olive tapenade

2 tsp dried oregano

2 garlic cloves, peeled +
    finely chopped

salt + pepper

a bunch of fresh basil
    (30g), roughly chopped

olive oil

1 Preheat the oven to 180°C fan/200°C/gas 6.

2 Put the pasta, Parmesan, courgettes, red peppers, tinned tomatoes, olive tapenade, oregano and garlic into a 30cm x 20cm deep roasting dish, along with generous pinches of salt and pepper and 500ml of hot water straight from a kettle. Stir to combine, then gently push the pasta down as far as you can into the water, cover the dish with a large baking tray or foil and roast for 45–55 minutes, stirring halfway through.

3 To finish, stir in the basil, then drizzle the pasta bake with olive oil and sprinkle with pepper and grated vegan Parmesan before serving.

FREEZER-FRIENDLY

ONE-DISH

PULLED AUBERGINE BÁNH MÌ

When an aubergine is roasted, the flesh becomes soft and creamy – ready to 'pull' into shreds and add to our favourite meals, like this Vietnamese-inspired sandwich. It's a great way to impress friends who think this decadent fruit is only ever rubbery and bitter.

EQUIPMENT: BAKING TRAY / BAKING PAPER / 2 SMALL BOWLS

SERVES 2 / PREP 10 MINS / COOK 35 MINS

2 aubergines

vegetable oil

1 tbsp dark soy sauce

3 tbsp hoisin sauce

2 garlic cloves, peeled + diced

1 carrot, thinly sliced

½ a cucumber, thinly sliced

½ a lime, juice only

½ tsp caster sugar

2 tbsp vegan mayonnaise

½ tbsp sriracha sauce

2 demi baguettes

a handful of fresh coriander (15g), leaves picked

1 Preheat the oven to 200°C fan/220°C/gas 7 and line a baking tray with baking paper. Slice the aubergines in half lengthways, then criss-cross the flesh side with a sharp knife and place them on the baking tray. Drizzle with oil and roast for 20–25 minutes, until very soft.

2 Use a fork to 'pull' the flesh from each aubergine half into shreds, discarding the skins. Transfer the pulled aubergine back to the baking tray, then stir in the soy sauce, hoisin sauce and garlic and drizzle with a little more oil. Spread the aubergine on the tray and roast for another 15 minutes.

3 Meanwhile, in a small bowl combine the carrot and cucumber with the lime juice and sugar. Combine the mayo and sriracha in a separate small bowl.

4 To build the bánh mì, slice the baguettes in half lengthways and fill them with the carrot and cucumber salad mix, then divide the pulled aubergine between the two sandwiches and finish with coriander leaves and a drizzle of the sriracha mayo.

GLUTEN-FREE (USE GF BAGUETTES, HOISIN + TAMARI)

HIGH IN PROTEIN

ONE-TRAY

RIPE TOMATO + MUSHROOM PASTA

Ripe tomatoes make all the difference to this fresh and simple pasta – they bring a more delicate flavour than tinned. Try to buy them in the hot summer months, when they're most ripe and therefore most fragrant.

EQUIPMENT: **BLENDER / FRYING PAN / SAUCEPAN**

SERVES **3–4** / PREP **10 MINS** / COOK **33 MINS**

1 slice of crusty bread

4 garlic cloves, peeled + finely chopped

2 sprigs of fresh thyme, leaves picked

olive oil

salt + pepper

400g chestnut mushrooms, sliced

500g ripe tomatoes, diced

2 tbsp balsamic vinegar

½ a vegetable stock cube

300g pasta (we use penne)

a handful of fresh basil leaves (10g)

1 Put the bread into a blender and blend until fine, then transfer the crumbs to a frying pan along with 1 chopped garlic clove, the thyme leaves, a drizzle of oil and pinches of salt and pepper. Fry for 3–5 minutes, or until golden, then tip out the crumb mixture on to a plate and set aside for later.

2 Wipe the pan clean, place it on a medium-high heat and add a drizzle of olive oil. Fry the mushrooms for 8 minutes, then add the remaining chopped garlic and fry for 2 minutes.

3 Add the tomatoes and balsamic vinegar, then crumble in the stock cube and stir to combine. Pop the lid on and leave the sauce to cook for 20 minutes, stirring occasionally.

4 Meanwhile, cook the pasta according to the packet instructions until al dente.

5 Tear the basil leaves into the sauce, leaving some for topping with later. Then use a slotted spoon to transfer the pasta straight into the sauce, adding some of the pasta water as you go to loosen it, and stir until combined. Season to taste with salt and pepper. To serve, top with the breadcrumbs and the rest of the basil leaves.

FREEZER-FRIENDLY (WITHOUT BREADCRUMBS)

GLUTEN-FREE (USE GF BREAD + PASTA)

JEWELLED PERSIAN RICE SALAD

Over the past couple of years we've loved exploring Persian cuisine – the subtle use of spices, the delicate flavours and of course the healthy obsession with rice. Golden-coloured turmeric is what gives this versatile dish its regal title, and it works just as well as a lunch, a light dinner or a tasty side to a bigger spread.

EQUIPMENT: **SAUCEPAN / FRYING PAN / LARGE MIXING BOWL**

SERVES **4** / PREP **20 MINS** / COOK **20 MINS**

200g quick-cook brown
    rice

½ tsp ground turmeric

salt + pepper

4 tbsp pine nuts

a large handful of fresh
    mint (20g), leaves
    picked

1 pomegranate

5 tbsp raisins

1 cucumber, sliced into
    rings

1 red onion, sliced

½ tsp ground cinnamon

2 tbsp olive oil

1 lemon, juice only

1 Put the rice, turmeric and a good pinch of salt into a saucepan. Add 550ml of water, cover with a lid and simmer for around 20–25 minutes, or until soft. If necessary, drain any excess liquid, then leave the rice to one side to cool.

2 Meanwhile, put the pine nuts into a frying pan on a medium-high heat and toast them for 2 minutes until golden, then transfer them to a large mixing bowl.

3 Tear the mint leaves into smaller pieces with your hands and add them to the mixing bowl (save a few leaves for serving later).

4 Cut the pomegranate in half and hit the skins to release all the seeds, then add the seeds to the mixing bowl along with the raisins, cucumber, red onion, cinnamon and the cooked rice. Add the olive oil and lemon juice, stir to combine and season to taste with salt and pepper before serving.

GLUTEN-FREE

CAVOLO NERO RISOTTO

If you can, you'll want to use a heavy-bottomed pan to make this risotto. This will help distribute the heat evenly and it'll withstand the constant stirring, which are both key to a creamy risotto. Curly kale will also work fine if you can't find cavolo nero. We usually save the stalks, cook them separately and add them to a soup.

EQUIPMENT: **SAUCEPAN / BLENDER / HIGH-SIDED PAN**

SERVES **4** / PREP **10 MINS** / COOK **32 MINS**

300g cavolo nero, stalks
   removed, leaves
   chopped

1 lemon, zest + juice

olive oil

1.2 litres vegetable stock

1 onion, peeled + finely
   chopped

5 garlic cloves, peeled +
   finely chopped

300g risotto rice (we
   use arborio)

200ml vegan dry
   white wine

50g vegan Parmesan,
   grated

1 Cook the cavolo nero leaves in a saucepan of boiling water for 3–4 minutes, until soft. Drain, then put into a blender along with the lemon zest and juice and 1 tablespoon of olive oil. Blend until smooth, like a purée, then leave to one side. Rinse out the saucepan, pour in the stock and bring to a very gentle boil.

2 Meanwhile, heat a little oil in a high-sided pan on a medium-high heat and fry the onion for 5 minutes. Add the garlic and fry for 2 minutes. Add the risotto rice and fry for another 2 minutes to toast the rice, then pour in the wine and keep stirring until it has reduced, around 5 minutes.

3 Add the hot stock a ladle at a time, stirring regularly until the rice is soft and the risotto texture is creamy (this should take around 15 minutes).

4 Stir in the cavolo nero purée and the grated Parmesan. Remove the risotto from the heat, cover and leave for a couple of minutes before serving with an extra drizzle of olive oil.

BUTTERNUT SQUASH + SAGE GALETTE

When we think of butternut squash, we often think of sage. They're a match made in heaven, and we put them to good use in this brilliant savoury galette. Simply serve with your favourite veggies, and don't forget you can store leftovers in the fridge for 2 or 3 days.

EQUIPMENT: SMALL BOWL / LARGE MIXING BOWL / ROASTING TRAY / BLENDER / BAKING TRAY / BAKING PAPER

SERVES 6 / PREP 15 MINS / COOK 55 MINS

80g cashews

1 butternut squash (1kg), peeled + diced, seeds reserved

olive oil

salt + pepper

12 fresh sage leaves

½ a lemon, juice only

6 tbsp plant-based milk (we use oat)

2 tbsp nutritional yeast

3 tbsp jarred caramelized onion

500g vegan shortcrust pastry

1 Preheat the oven to 200°C fan/220°C/gas 7. Put the cashews into a small bowl and soak them in hot water straight from a kettle.

2 Meanwhile, put the diced butternut squash into a large mixing bowl along with a generous drizzle of olive oil and pinches of salt and pepper. Toss through, then transfer to a roasting tray and roast for 15 minutes.

3 Toss the sage leaves in the same large bowl with a splash of oil, then add them to the roasting tray and roast with the squash for another 10 minutes.

4 Meanwhile, rinse and drain the squash seeds, then leave to one side for later.

5 Drain the cashews and put them into a blender with the lemon juice, plant-based milk, nutritional yeast and pinches of salt and pepper. Blend until smooth.

6 Once the butternut squash is ready, add the caramelized onion to the tray and stir through with a spoon.

7 Line a baking tray with baking paper. Roll out the pastry to a circle about 35cm in diameter and place it on the tray. Spread the cashew sauce over the middle of the pastry, leaving a 4cm border around the edge. Spoon the butternut squash over the top of the cashew sauce and top with the reserved seeds. Fold the edges of the pastry over the filling, overlapping the pastry as you go. Brush the pastry edges with oil and sprinkle them with salt. Bake for 30 minutes, or until the crust is golden brown.

GLUTEN-FREE (USE GF PASTRY)

HARISSA BOLOGNESE

Rose harissa paste has a more subtle heat than regular harissa, and you should be able to find it in most large supermarkets. It totally reinvents this classic pasta, giving it a spicy and smoky kick – and you can also put it to good use in our Harissa Aubergine (page 93) or Stuffed Courgettes (page 136).

EQUIPMENT: **LARGE CASSEROLE POT OR LARGE SAUCEPAN / SAUCEPAN**

SERVES **6** / PREP **10 MINS** / COOK **37 MINS**

olive oil

1 onion, peeled + finely
   chopped

2 celery stalks, chopped

2 carrots, diced

4 garlic cloves, peeled +
   finely chopped

2 sprigs of fresh rosemary,
   leaves picked +
   chopped

200ml vegan red wine

2 x 400g tins of green
   lentils, drained + rinsed

2 x 400g tins of chopped
   tomatoes

4 tbsp rose harissa paste

salt + pepper

450g pasta (we use
   mafaldine)

1 Heat a drizzle of oil in a large casserole pot or large saucepan over a medium heat. Add the onions, celery and carrots and fry for 8 minutes. Add the garlic and rosemary and fry for 2 minutes.

2 Pour in the wine and cook for 2 minutes, then add the lentils, tinned tomatoes, rose harissa paste and pinches of salt and pepper. Bring the bolognese to the boil, then reduce the heat and simmer for 25 minutes.

3 Meanwhile, cook the pasta according to the packet instructions until al dente.

4 Once the bolognese sauce is ready, use a slotted spoon to transfer the pasta straight into the sauce, adding some of the pasta water as you go to loosen it, then stir well and season to taste with more salt and pepper before serving.

FREEZER-FRIENDLY

GLUTEN-FREE (USE GF PASTA)

SLOPPY JOE QUESADILLAS

Sloppy Joe is usually made with minced beef and Worcestershire sauce. Our version features a more planet-friendly combo of lentils and a choice blend of spices, along with the more traditional tomato sauce. Here we layer the mixture inside our epic cheesy quesadillas, but you can also add it to burger buns or even tacos.

EQUIPMENT: **2 FRYING PANS**

SERVES **6** / PREP **7 MINS** / COOK **32 MINS**

olive oil

1 onion, peeled + diced

3 garlic cloves, peeled + chopped

2 x 400g tins of green lentils, drained + rinsed

2 tbsp tomato purée

400ml passata

1 tsp smoked paprika

½ tsp chilli flakes, plus extra

1 tsp ground cumin

2 tsp caster sugar

salt + pepper

6 tortillas

200g vegan cheese, grated (we use Cheddar style)

1 Drizzle some oil into a frying pan on a medium-high heat. Add the onion and fry for 8 minutes. Then add the garlic and fry for 1 minute.

2 Stir in the lentils, tomato purée, passata, spices, sugar and pinches of salt and pepper. Bring the mixture to a simmer, then cook for 10 minutes.

3 Once the mixture is ready, put a tortilla into a clean frying pan on a medium heat. Sprinkle a third of the cheese over the tortilla, then add a third of the sloppy Joe and spread all over. Cover with a second tortilla. Fry for 2–3 minutes on each side (be sure to flip carefully), or until golden and crispy, then remove the quesadilla from the pan and repeat with the remaining 2 quesadillas.

4 Cut the quesadillas into 6 triangles, finish with a drizzle of oil and top with a few more chilli flakes before serving.

FREEZER-FRIENDLY (LENTIL MIXTURE ONLY)

GLUTEN-FREE (USE GF TORTILLAS)

FRENCH ONION + MUSHROOM STEW
WITH GARLIC BREAD

Ben inherited a love for cooking from his dad – whose signature dishes included a comforting casserole topped with garlic bread, which would soak up the rich sauce while the top half turned crispy and golden brown. If you don't have an ovenproof pan, you can simply cook everything in a regular pan, then transfer the stew to an ovenproof dish and continue with step 4.

EQUIPMENT: **DEEP OVENPROOF PAN / SMALL BOWL**

SERVES **4** / PREP **10 MINS** / COOK **54 MINS**

4 tbsp vegan butter or
    margarine
600g chestnut mushrooms
4 large onions (1kg),
    peeled + finely sliced
salt + pepper
3 sprigs of fresh thyme,
    leaves picked
2 bay leaves
6 garlic cloves, peeled +
    finely chopped
2 tbsp plain flour
200ml vegan dry
    white wine
500ml vegetable stock
1 tsp caster sugar
1 large baguette
a small handful of fresh
    parsley (10g), chopped

1 Put 1 tablespoon of butter into a deep ovenproof pan on a medium-high heat, then add the mushrooms and fry them whole for 10 minutes, or until no liquid remains and they begin to brown. Remove the mushrooms from the pan and set to one side.

2 Add another tablespoon of butter to the pan and fry the onions with a pinch of salt for 8–10 minutes, or until brown. Add the thyme leaves, bay leaves and 4 of the garlic cloves, then reduce the heat to low and cook for 20 minutes, stirring occasionally.

3 Add the flour and cook for 1 minute. Turn up the heat, pour in the wine and let it cook for 2 minutes. Add the stock and sugar, as well as the mushrooms from earlier, and let the stew bubble away for 10 minutes or until the sauce has thickened.

4 Meanwhile, cut the baguette into 2cm thick slices. Combine 2 tablespoons of butter with the remaining 2 garlic cloves and the chopped parsley to make a garlic and parsley butter, and spread it on one side of the slices of bread. Lay the bread on top of the stew, buttered side up, and grill for 3–5 minutes, or until the bread is golden.

FREEZER-FRIENDLY (WITHOUT GARLIC BREAD)
GLUTEN-FREE (USE GF FLOUR + BAGUETTE)
ONE-PAN

TOMATO + FENNEL MACARONI SOUP

A family favourite. Roxy's love affair with soups was passed down by her Polish mum. Like her mum, you'll almost always find Roxy in the kitchen testing a new 'zupa', such as this simple take using delicate fennel, fresh tomatoes and macaroni – the last of which you can switch for whatever pasta you like (we often use orzo).

EQUIPMENT: **LARGE CASSEROLE POT OR LARGE SAUCEPAN / HANDHELD BLENDER**

SERVES **4–6** / PREP **15 MINS** / COOK **25 MINS**

olive oil

1 onion, peeled + thinly
  sliced

2 fennel bulbs

6 garlic cloves, peeled +
  thinly sliced

1kg ripe tomatoes, roughly
  chopped

1 litre vegetable stock

200g macaroni

salt + pepper

crusty bread, to serve

1 Heat a generous drizzle of oil in a large casserole pot or large saucepan on a medium heat. Once hot, fry the onion for 5 minutes. Meanwhile, cut the fennel bulbs in half and thinly slice the flesh, saving the fronds to decorate with later.

2 Add the fennel, garlic and tomatoes to the casserole pot or saucepan and fry for 10 minutes. Then pour in the stock and blend the soup until smooth.

3 Add the macaroni to the soup and simmer for 10 minutes, or until the pasta is ready. Taste and season with salt and pepper to your liking.

4 Serve the soup with a drizzle of oil, freshly ground black pepper, and the reserved fennel fronds for an extra burst of fennel flavour, with a side of crusty bread.

FREEZER-FRIENDLY

GLUTEN-FREE (USE GF PASTA + BREAD)

ONE-POT

PEANUT BUTTER AUBERGINE + SMACKED CUCUMBER

Smacking a cucumber might seem a bit daft, but it's a technique that originates from China and it helps tenderize the vegetable. This in turn helps it soak up flavour, to create the perfect topping for our peanut butter aubergine, which we enjoy as a lunch or a light dinner.

EQUIPMENT: LARGE ROASTING TRAY / MIXING BOWL / SMALL BOWL

SERVES **4** / PREP **5 MINS** / COOK **35 MINS**

4 aubergines

olive oil

salt + pepper

1 cucumber

1 tsp chilli oil

2 tbsp light soy sauce

1 lime

120g smooth peanut butter

2 tbsp maple syrup

2 spring onions, sliced

1 Preheat the oven to 200°C fan/220°C/gas 7.

2 Slice the aubergines in half lengthways, then criss-cross the flesh side with a sharp knife and put them on a large roasting tray. Drizzle a little oil over the cut sides, sprinkle with salt and pepper, and roast for 30 minutes.

3 Meanwhile, smack the cucumber with a rolling pin or the bottom of a saucepan until squashed, then slice it into bite-size pieces and put them into a mixing bowl along with ½ teaspoon of chilli oil, 1 tablespoon of light soy sauce and the juice of half the lime. Stir, then leave to one side.

4 In a small bowl combine the peanut butter with 1 tablespoon of light soy sauce, the maple syrup, the juice of the remaining half lime and 5 tablespoons of water.

5 Remove the aubergines from the oven. Brush the peanut sauce all over the aubergine halves, making sure most of the sauce makes its way into the grooves, then roast for another 5 minutes.

6 To serve, top the aubergine with the smacked cucumber and sliced spring onions and drizzle over the remaining ½ teaspoon of chilli oil.

GLUTEN-FREE (USE TAMARI)

ONE-TRAY

BEETROOT, CHICORY + WHIPPED FETA SALAD

UK-grown beetroots are available almost all year round, but they are most tender (and sweetest) in the summer months. We love pairing their distinctive earthy flavour with tangy vegan feta, which we blitz in a food processor with yoghurt to create a silky smooth dressing.

EQUIPMENT: **ROASTING TRAY / FOOD PROCESSOR**

SERVES **6** / PREP **10 MINS** / COOK **28 MINS**

400g raw beetroot, peeled
+ sliced into wedges

olive oil

salt + pepper

80g walnuts

150g vegan feta, roughly
cubed

150g vegan yoghurt (we
use oat Greek style)

1 lemon, juice only

250g red chicory

2 red apples, cores
removed, sliced into thin
wedges

a handful of fresh dill (15g),
roughly chopped

1 Preheat the oven to 200°C fan/220°C/gas 7. Place the beetroot on a roasting tray and drizzle with olive oil, then sprinkle with salt and pepper. Toss to combine and roast for 25 minutes. Then remove the tray from the oven, add the walnuts, and roast everything together for another 3–5 minutes, or until the beetroot is soft but has some bite to it and the walnuts are toasted.

2 Meanwhile, to prepare the feta dressing, put the feta, yoghurt and the juice from half the lemon into a food processor until smooth, scraping down the sides as you go. Taste and adjust the seasoning to your liking.

3 Slice off the bottom third of the chicory, then pick the leaves, rinse them and pat them dry. Arrange the leaves on a serving plate and place the beetroot and apples on top. Sprinkle the dill all over, along with pinches of salt and pepper.

4 Dollop most of the feta dressing over the top and distribute the walnuts evenly. Finish with a drizzle of olive oil and the juice from the remaining half lemon. Transfer the rest of the whipped feta to a small bowl and serve alongside.

GLUTEN-FREE
ONE-TRAY

JAMAICAN TOFU CURRY

There's nothing we love more than scooping up chunks of this vibrant Jamaican curry and coleslaw with torn pieces of roti. We prefer to use a mild curry powder, or those labelled 'Jamaican', which are less spicy and more fragrant.

EQUIPMENT: MIXING BOWL / LARGE NON-STICK FRYING PAN

SERVES 4 / PREP 15 MINS / COOK 30 MINS

200g red cabbage, finely sliced

200g white cabbage, finely sliced

1 lemon, juice only

salt + pepper

400g block of extra firm tofu, drained

2 tbsp cornflour

2 tsp mild curry powder

vegetable oil

1 onion, peeled + finely chopped

3 garlic cloves, peeled + finely chopped

½ a thumb of fresh ginger (15g), peeled + finely chopped

½ tsp ground allspice

2 tomatoes, roughly chopped

2 Scotch bonnet chillies

4 tbsp vegan mayonnaise

4 rotis

1 Put the red cabbage and white cabbage into a mixing bowl and add the lemon juice and pinches of salt and pepper. Toss to combine, then leave to sit while you carry out the next steps.

2 Tear the tofu into bite-size pieces. On a plate, combine the cornflour with 1 teaspoon of curry powder and generous pinches of salt and pepper. Coat the tofu pieces in the cornflour mixture on all sides. Heat a little oil in a large non-stick frying pan on a medium-high heat and fry the tofu for 8 minutes, until golden, then transfer the tofu to a plate.

3 Add a little more oil to the pan and fry the onion, garlic and ginger for 3 minutes. Add the remaining 1 teaspoon of curry powder along with the allspice and fry for 1 minute, then add the tomatoes and fry for 3 minutes.

4 Now add the Scotch bonnets (we add them whole, which brings a lovely aroma to the curry without adding too much heat), along with 400ml of water and generous pinches of salt and pepper, and leave the curry to simmer on a low heat for 15 minutes. Then stir the tofu back in, remove the pan from the heat and discard the Scotch bonnets.

5 Finally, stir the mayonnaise into the coleslaw and serve alongside the curry and rotis.

FREEZER-FRIENDLY (CURRY ONLY)

GLUTEN-FREE (USE GF ROTI)

HIGH IN PROTEIN

ONE-POT

ROXY'S BIGOS

Bigos, also known as hunter's stew, is one of Roxy's favourite Polish dishes and it's something she has very fond memories of eating as a child. It's a hearty meal that leaves a warm feeling in your tummy – both figuratively and literally. Juniper berries are sold dried and you'll find them among the herbs and spices, but if you prefer, you can substitute a few sprigs of fresh rosemary. Bigos will always taste better over time, so make the most of any leftovers the following day.

EQUIPMENT: **LARGE CASSEROLE POT OR LARGE SAUCEPAN**

SERVES **4–6** / PREP **5 MINS** / COOK **52 MINS**

olive oil

8 vegan sausages (we use chorizo style)

1 onion, peeled + sliced

300g closed cup mushrooms, sliced

3 bay leaves

½ tsp caraway seeds

1 tsp juniper berries, crushed

1 tsp smoked paprika

1 x 400g tin of chopped tomatoes

1 litre vegetable stock

600g sauerkraut

400g white cabbage, finely sliced

2 tbsp tomato purée

salt + pepper

a handful of fresh parsley (15g), roughly chopped

crusty bread, to serve

1 Heat a little oil in a large casserole pot or large saucepan on a medium-high heat and fry the sausages for 5 minutes or until charred. Remove the sausages, leaving all their juices in the pot, then slice them into thirds and set aside.

2 Add another drizzle of oil to the same pot on a medium-high heat and fry the onion for 5 minutes, or until translucent. Add the mushrooms and fry for another 10 minutes, or until they begin to brown.

3 Add the bay leaves, caraway seeds, juniper berries and paprika and fry for 2 minutes. Add the tomatoes, stock, sauerkraut, cabbage, tomato purée and sausages, and season with salt and pepper. Bring the bigos to the boil, then reduce the heat and simmer on medium for 30 minutes.

4 To finish, serve in bowls, sprinkle over some chopped parsley and dunk in slices of crusty bread.

FREEZER-FRIENDLY

GLUTEN-FREE (USE GF BREAD)

ONE-POT

MOROCCAN-STYLE SQUASH + CHICKPEA STEW

In our home, autumn is synonymous with butternut squash. As soon as summer ends, there's a steady supply of squash on hand to throw into curries, pies and stews. This Moroccan-inspired stew incorporates flavours we love from the region, including aromatic spices, apricots, olives and lemon. We sometimes serve this as part of a wider spread, or just tuck in with crusty bread and lettuce.

EQUIPMENT: BAKING TRAY / SAUCEPAN

SERVES 4 / PREP 10 MINS / COOK 32 MINS

1 butternut squash

olive oil

salt + pepper

1 tsp ground cinnamon

1 onion, peeled + finely
  sliced

8 cardamom pods, seeds
  chopped or crushed

5 garlic cloves, peeled +
  finely chopped

2 tsp cumin seeds

2 x 400g tins of chopped
  tomatoes

2 x 400g tins of chickpeas,
  drained + rinsed

12 dried apricots, roughly
  chopped

80g pitted green olives in
  brine, plus 4 tbsp brine

½ a lemon, juice only

a handful of fresh mint
  (15g), leaves picked

1 Preheat the oven to 180°C fan/200°C/gas 6. Peel the butternut squash, then cut it in half lengthways, remove the seeds and slice the flesh into 1cm thick rings. Put the squash slices on a baking tray, drizzle with olive oil, and sprinkle with salt and pepper and the cinnamon. Toss to combine, then roast for 30 minutes or until soft.

2 Meanwhile, heat a little oil in a saucepan and fry the onion for 5 minutes. Add the crushed cardamom seeds, garlic and cumin seeds, and cook for 2 minutes.

3 Add the tinned tomatoes, then rinse out the tins with a splash of water and add the water to the pan. Add the chickpeas and apricots, bring the stew to the boil, then reduce to a low simmer and cook for 25 minutes.

4 Stir in the olives, along with 4 tablespoons of brine from the jar, and add the lemon juice. To serve, top the roasted butternut squash with the stew and sprinkle the mint leaves all over.

FREEZER-FRIENDLY

GLUTEN-FREE

CHICKPEA + SPINACH SAMOSA ROLLS

The filling for these samosa rolls is inspired by one of our favourite curries, chana saag, which involves cooking chickpeas and spinach in a gently spiced sauce. The end result is a devilishly moreish combination of fluffy pastry, fragrant curry and sweet mango chutney. Yum!

EQUIPMENT: **FRYING PAN / BAKING TRAY / BAKING PAPER**

MAKES **8 ROLLS** / PREP **10 MINS** / COOK **28 MINS**

vegetable oil

1 shallot, peeled + finely chopped

2 garlic cloves, peeled + finely chopped

1 tsp garam masala

½ tsp fennel seeds

½ x 400g tin of chickpeas, drained + rinsed

2 tbsp tomato purée

80g baby spinach

80g frozen peas

salt + pepper

1 x 320g sheet of vegan puff pastry

2 tbsp mango chutney, plus extra

1 Heat a little oil in a frying pan on a medium heat and fry the shallot and garlic for 2 minutes. Add the garam masala and fennel seeds and fry for 1 minute. Tip in the chickpeas, then half-fill the tin with water and pour it into the pan, followed by the tomato purée. Cook for 3 minutes, crushing the chickpeas with the back of a wooden spoon as you go until they're mostly broken down.

2 Add the spinach, frozen peas and generous pinches of salt and pepper. Cook for 2 minutes, or until the spinach has wilted and there is no moisture left in the mixture. Transfer the mixture to a plate and leave to cool.

3 Meanwhile, preheat the oven to 180°C fan/200°C/gas 6 and line a baking tray with baking paper. Roll out the sheet of puff pastry so the longest side faces you, and spread the mango chutney all over. Once the chickpea filling has cooled, spread the filling across the pastry, leaving a 2cm border, then, starting at the longest edge, roll tightly into a long log like a Swiss roll. Slice the log into 8 rolls and place them on the lined baking tray cut side up, 2cm apart. Bake for 20–25 minutes, or until golden.

4 Remove the rolls from the oven, brush the tops with a little more chutney and serve.

FREEZER-FRIENDLY

GLUTEN-FREE (USE GF PASTRY)

CHEESY LEEK + ARTICHOKE CHILLI TART

Shop-bought pastry is a life-saver when it comes to cooking fuss-free meals at home, and savoury tarts are one of the easiest (and most delicious) ways to put it to good use. Our method is always the same: layer with a relish or chutney, follow with a cheesy base, then top with vegetables. Relish is generally less sweet than chutney, but we often use them interchangeably.

EQUIPMENT: **BAKING PAPER / BAKING TRAY / FRYING PAN**

SERVES **4** / PREP **10 MINS** / COOK **25 MINS**

1 x 320g sheet of vegan
   puff pastry

2 tbsp vegan butter or
   margarine

2 tbsp plain flour

250ml plant-based milk
   (we use oat)

50g vegan cheese, finely
   grated (we use Cheddar
   style)

150g jarred artichokes,
   quartered

1 leek, thinly sliced into
   rings

salt + pepper

2 tbsp chilli relish or chilli
   chutney

1 Preheat the oven to 200°C fan/220°C/gas 7. Unroll the sheet of puff pastry, keeping it on its baking paper, and place it on a large baking tray. Score a 1cm border round all the edge of the pastry and prick the middle section a few times with a fork, then bake for 10 minutes.

2 For the cheesy béchamel sauce, melt the butter in a frying pan on a medium heat, then add the flour and stir for 1–2 minutes with a wooden spoon until combined. Pour in the milk and keep stirring until the sauce is smooth and has thickened – this will take around 5–8 minutes (you can use a whisk to break down any lumps of flour). Add most of the vegan cheese to the sauce and stir until melted, then remove the pan from the heat.

3 Slice any thick artichoke quarters in half, then stir all of them into the cheese sauce along with the leeks and pinches of salt and pepper.

4 If the middle section of the puff pastry has puffed up, push it down gently. Spread the chilli relish across the pastry, keeping it within the border, then spread the cheesy filling on top. Bake for 10–15 minutes, or until the pastry is golden brown, then slice into 4 to serve.

FREEZER-FRIENDLY

GLUTEN-FREE (USE GF PASTRY + FLOUR)

ROASTED BUTTERNUT SQUASH DHAL
WITH CRISPY SHALLOTS

Our daughter Maya is totally obsessed with dhal and we create versions of it for her all the time, including this take using roasted butternut squash. Often we'll serve it with warm roti or naan, or we'll happily eat it as is for lunch.

EQUIPMENT: LARGE ROASTING TRAY / SMALL SAUCEPAN / LARGE CASSEROLE POT OR LARGE SAUCEPAN

SERVES **4** / PREP **15 MINS** / COOK **29 MINS**

1 butternut squash (1.1kg), peeled + diced

vegetable oil

salt + pepper

1 tsp fennel seeds

3 shallots, peeled + thinly sliced

6 garlic cloves, peeled + finely chopped

a thumb of fresh ginger, peeled + finely chopped

1 tbsp cumin seeds

2 green chillies

4 ripe tomatoes, roughly chopped

1 tsp ground turmeric

2 tsp garam masala

350g red lentils

1 Preheat the oven to 180°C fan/200°C/gas 6. Put the diced butternut squash on a large roasting tray, drizzle with vegetable oil, and sprinkle with salt, pepper and the fennel seeds. Toss, then roast for 25 minutes or until soft.

2 Drizzle a generous glug of vegetable oil into a small saucepan so it covers the base. Add 2 of the shallots to the pan along with a pinch of salt, and place the pan on a low-medium heat. Fry for 10 minutes, or until the shallots are brown and crispy, then transfer them to a plate and set aside.

3 Put the garlic, ginger, cumin seeds and the remaining shallot into a large casserole pot or large saucepan. Pierce the chillies a few times each and throw them into the pan, then fry everything for 2 minutes. Add the tomatoes, turmeric and garam masala, then stir and cook for 5 minutes.

4 Add the lentils along with 1.2 litres of hot water from a kettle. Bring the dhal to the boil, then reduce the heat and simmer for 10–15 minutes.

5 To finish, stir the butternut squash into the dhal, season to taste with salt and top with the crispy shallots.

FREEZER-FRIENDLY
GLUTEN-FREE
HIGH IN PROTEIN

DESSERTS

GOOEY CHOCOLATE BROWNIES

Chocolate brownies are one of the vital building blocks for a happy life. At least that's what we've convinced ourselves. These tried-and-tested brownies deliver on exactly what you want from a brownie – a gloriously gooey middle, surrounded by a sweet and sticky cake.

**EQUIPMENT: SQUARE BAKING TIN / BAKING PAPER / JUG /
SMALL SAUCEPAN / LARGE MIXING BOWL**

MAKES **9 BROWNIES** / PREP **10 MINS** / COOK **33 MINS** + **15 MINS** COOLING

150ml unsweetened soy milk

1 tbsp apple cider vinegar

180g 70% vegan dark chocolate, roughly chopped

100g vegan butter or margarine

300g caster sugar

120g plain flour

80g cocoa powder

salt

1 Preheat the oven to 160°C fan/180°C/gas 4 and line the base and sides of an approx. 20cm square baking tin with baking paper, making sure the paper comes to the top of the tin.

2 Combine the soy milk and apple cider vinegar in a jug, then leave to one side. The milk will curdle to create your vegan buttermilk.

3 Put the dark chocolate and vegan butter into a small saucepan over a low heat and cook for 3–5 minutes or until melted, stirring occasionally, then remove from the heat.

4 In a large mixing bowl combine the sugar, flour and cocoa powder with a pinch of salt. Pour in the melted chocolate mixture and vegan buttermilk, and mix until smooth. Transfer the brownie mixture to the prepared baking tin and level it out with a spatula.

5 Bake for 30–35 minutes, or until a little of the batter still sticks to a skewer when you insert it into the brownie. Then leave to cool slightly for 15 minutes before pulling the brownies out of the tin using the baking paper and slicing into 9 squares. Store in an airtight container and they'll keep for 3–4 days at room temperature or one week in the fridge.

SPICED APPLE TRAYBAKE PANCAKE

Pancakes aren't always the most convenient option, especially when you have many mouths to feed. This traybake version – affectionately known as the 'giant' pancake in our household – takes the fuss out of flipping pancakes. If you prefer, you can use the pancake mix as a base and experiment with your own toppings.

EQUIPMENT: BAKING DISH / JUG / SAUCEPAN / LARGE MIXING BOWL

SERVES 12 / PREP 10 MINS / COOK 25 MINS

6 tbsp vegan butter or
   margarine, plus extra
   for greasing

400ml unsweetened soy
   milk

1 lemon, juice only

5 red apples

6 tbsp maple syrup, plus
   extra for serving

½ tsp ground cinnamon

250g plain flour, plus extra

1 tbsp baking powder

salt

½ tbsp vanilla extract

vegan ice cream, to serve
   (optional)

1 Preheat the oven to 180°C fan/200°C/gas 6 and grease the base and sides of an approx. 28cm x 20cm baking dish with vegan butter.

2 In a jug combine the soy milk and lemon juice, then leave to one side. The milk will curdle to create your vegan buttermilk.

3 Remove the cores from the apples and slice the flesh into 1cm thick wedges. Put the butter, 5 tablespoons of maple syrup and the cinnamon into a saucepan on a medium heat, and cook for a few minutes until melted and combined. Stir in the sliced apples and simmer for 6 minutes, or until the apples are mostly soft, then stir in 2 teaspoons of flour and cook for another 2 minutes, or until the sauce has thickened.

4 In a large mixing bowl combine the rest of the flour, the baking powder and a small pinch of salt. Then pour in the vanilla extract, along with the remaining 1 tablespoon of maple syrup and the vegan buttermilk, and combine.

5 Pour the pancake batter into the prepared tin. Using a fork, pick out the apples from the saucepan and lay them all over the pancake mixture, leaving the caramel in the saucepan to use later. Bake the pancake for 15 minutes.

6 Pour the remaining caramel all over the pancake and, if you like, serve with more maple syrup and vegan ice cream. Wrap and store leftovers in an airtight container for 2–3 days in the fridge, or freeze for up to 1 month.

STRAWBERRY DUMP CAKE

Dump cake is an American invention, and literally means 'dumping' the ingredients into a dish. We forgive the Americans for not knowing how it might sound on this side of the pond – but regardless of what it's called, this no-fuss pud couldn't be any easier, and the combo of fresh strawberries, fluffy cake and vegan ice cream is all we could ever dream of.

EQUIPMENT: **BAKING DISH / MIXING BOWL / SMALL SAUCEPAN**

SERVES **6** / PREP **10 MINS** / COOK **25 MINS**

650g strawberries, tops removed, halved

1 lemon, juice only

1½ tbsp cornflour

1½ tbsp strawberry jam

180g plain flour

100g caster sugar

1 tsp baking powder

170g vegan butter or margarine

1 tbsp vanilla extract

vegan vanilla ice cream, to serve

1 Preheat the oven to 180°C fan/200°C/gas 6.

2 Toss the strawberries, lemon juice, cornflour and jam into an approx. 22cm x 33cm baking dish and stir until fully combined.

3 In a mixing bowl combine the flour, sugar and baking powder. Melt the butter either in a microwave or in a small saucepan, add the vanilla extract, and pour it over the dry ingredients. Mix until combined, then spoon the cake mixture over the strawberries and use the back of a spoon to spread it evenly.

4 Bake for 25–30 minutes, or until golden and the filling is bubbling. Leave for a few minutes, then serve with dollops of ice cream. Store leftovers in an airtight container for 2–3 days in the fridge, or freeze for up to a month.

FREEZER-FRIENDLY

GLUTEN-FREE (USE GF FLOUR)

SUMMER FRUITS + CHIA TART

You can use this wonderful tart as a template for whatever fruit you like. Simply bake the pastry, add the chia yoghurt and top with anything from banana to kiwi, mango, grapes – or whatever it is you need to use up.

EQUIPMENT: SMALL BOWL / LARGE BAKING TRAY / BAKING PAPER

SERVES **8** / PREP **10 MINS** / COOK **10 MINS** + **20 MINS** COOLING

2 tsp chia seeds

½ tbsp vanilla extract

240g vegan yoghurt
   (we use oat)

1 tbsp maple syrup,
   plus extra

1 x 320g sheet of vegan
   puff pastry

3 ripe nectarines, halved +
   sliced into 1cm wedges

150g mixed berries (we use
   strawberries, blueberries
   + raspberries)

a few fresh mint leaves

1   Preheat the oven to 180°C fan/200°C/gas 6.

2   In a small bowl combine the chia seeds with the vanilla extract, yoghurt and maple syrup. Stir, then pop into the fridge while you complete the next steps.

3   Roll out the pastry on a large baking tray, keeping it on its baking paper (trim the baking paper to fit the tray, if necessary). Score a border of 1cm all around the pastry and make several incisions in the centre with a knife so the steam can escape. Brush the pastry all over with maple syrup and bake for 10–15 minutes, or until golden brown.

4   Once the pastry is ready, push it down in the middle if it has puffed up, and leave to cool.

5   Spread the chia yoghurt all over the pastry, keeping it within the border, then top with the fruit and finish with an extra drizzle of maple syrup and a sprinkling of mint leaves. This is best eaten immediately, but you can store leftovers in an airtight container in the fridge for 1–2 days.

GLUTEN-FREE (USE GF PASTRY)

ONE-TRAY

CELEBRATION CAKE

We get asked a lot for birthday cake recipes, so we knew we needed to bring a showstopper celebration cake to this cookbook. This soft and fluffy coconut-flavoured cake is smothered in buttercream, then topped with colourful fruits. Be sure to give the tin of coconut milk a good shake before opening, because often the cream and water will separate in the tin.

EQUIPMENT: 2 CAKE TINS / BAKING PAPER / LARGE MIXING BOWL / WHISK

SERVES 16 / PREP 20 MINS / COOK 25 MINS + 2 HRS COOLING

100g vegan margarine,
   plus extra for greasing

300g plain flour

120g desiccated coconut

250g caster sugar

1½ tsp baking powder

½ tsp bicarbonate of soda

300ml tinned full-fat
   coconut milk

100ml coconut oil, melted

1 lemon, zest + juice

450g icing sugar,
   plus extra

selection of fruit (we
   use plums, apricots,
   kiwi, raspberries +
   blueberries)

1 Preheat the oven to 180°C fan/200°C/gas 6. Grease two 20cm cake tins with vegan margarine and line the bases with baking paper.

2 Put the flour, desiccated coconut, sugar, baking powder and bicarbonate of soda into a large mixing bowl and stir. Add the coconut milk, oil, the zest of the whole lemon and 1 tablespoon of lemon juice and stir to combine.

3 Pour the cake batter into the prepared cake tins and bake for 25–30 minutes, or until firm and a skewer inserted comes out clean. Leave the cakes to cool for 15 minutes in the tins, then turn them out on to a cooling rack and leave to cool completely.

4 Meanwhile, to prepare the buttercream, put the vegan margarine, icing sugar and 1 tablespoon of lemon juice into a bowl and whisk until smooth and light. If the buttercream is too soft, add a little more icing sugar.

5 Once the cakes have cooled, place one in the middle of a serving plate and spread half the buttercream over the top. Then place the second cake on top and spread the remaining buttercream all over it. To finish, remove any stones from the fruits and slice, then place all the fruit on top of the cake. You can store leftover slices of cake (without the fruit) at room temperature for a couple of days. Alternatively, wrap and store in an airtight container in the fridge for 5 days, or freeze for up to 1 month.

FREEZER-FRIENDLY (WITHOUT FRUIT)

GLUTEN-FREE (USE GF FLOUR)

AFFOGATO + HAZELNUT BRITTLE

Affogato al caffè is an Italian dessert usually enjoyed during the summer months. It's a simple but effective combo of ice-cold gelato and hot espresso. As such you'll want to enjoy it relatively quickly, so for our version make sure the delicious hazelnut brittle is ready before serving. Also be sure your saucepan is smaller than the hob top so that the sugar heats and dissolves evenly.

EQUIPMENT: BAKING TRAY / BAKING PAPER / SMALL SAUCEPAN

SERVES 4 / PREP 10 MINS / COOK 5 MINS + 30 MINS COOLING

olive oil

100g caster sugar

2 tbsp hazelnuts

8 scoops of vegan vanilla ice cream

4 shots of coffee (30ml each)

10g 70% vegan dark chocolate, roughly chopped

1 Line a baking tray with baking paper and grease the paper with a little oil.

2 Put the sugar and 1 tablespoon of water into a small saucepan off the heat and stir to combine. Then pop the pan on a medium heat and leave to cook for 5–10 minutes. Don't stir or touch the caramel, just swirl the pan around occasionally. Over time the caramel should become liquid and bubble. Once the caramel has turned a golden colour, tip in the whole hazelnuts and stir with a spatula. Pour the caramel on to the baking paper and ease it out to a few millimetres thick, using the spatula. Leave to cool so that it hardens.

3 Once hard, bash the brittle with a rolling pin to break it into smaller pieces.

4 Put a scoop of ice cream into each serving glass, along with a shot of hot coffee. Top with a couple of pieces of the brittle and some pieces of chocolate. Serve straight away.

MERINGUES + CARAMELIZED BANANAS

Aquafaba is the juice from a tin of chickpeas and it conveniently doubles up as egg white. These delightful meringues can be made ahead of time – just be sure to store them in an airtight container and separate them from each other with baking paper to stop them sticking together. They'll keep for 2–3 days at room temperature.

EQUIPMENT: LARGE BAKING TRAY / BAKING PAPER / MIXING BOWL / HANDHELD ELECTRIC WHISK / FRYING PAN

SERVES **4** / PREP **15 MINS** / COOK **2 HRS** + **20 MINS** COOLING

4 tbsp aquafaba

45g + 1 tbsp caster sugar

2 bananas

¼ tsp ground cinnamon

1 tbsp vegan butter or margarine

2 tbsp coconut flakes

8 tbsp vegan yoghurt (we use coconut)

maple syrup, to serve

1 Preheat the oven to 100°C fan/120°C/gas ½. Line a large baking tray with baking paper.

2 Put the aquafaba into a mixing bowl and whisk with a handheld electric whisk for 5 minutes, or until white and fluffy. Then add the 45g of sugar a tablespoon at a time and continue whisking for another 5 minutes, until you get stiff and glossy peaks.

3 Spoon the meringue mixture on to the lined baking tray to make 12 small meringues. Bake for 2 hours.

4 Meanwhile, peel the bananas and slice them into rings. Sprinkle the remaining 1 tablespoon of sugar over both sides, along with the cinnamon. Heat the butter in a frying pan on a medium heat, then add the bananas and fry for 3–5 minutes on each side, or until golden brown and caramelized. Transfer the bananas to a plate and leave to cool.

5 Wipe out the pan and place it on a medium heat. Toast the coconut flakes for 3–5 minutes, or until golden, then leave them to one side to cool.

6 Once the meringues are ready, place 3 on each serving plate and top with vegan yoghurt, the caramelized bananas, a drizzle of maple syrup and the toasted coconut flakes. Serve straight away.

CHOCOLATE ORANGE + TAHINI FRIDGE CAKE

Tahini is a staple in our household, and you'll find us adding it to anything from noodles (page 29) to Tofu Lahmacun (page 90) – as well as fuss-free desserts like this fridge cake. It brings a rich and nutty flavour, similar to peanut butter but more subtle, and works perfectly mixed with the sweet orange-flavoured chocolate.

EQUIPMENT: **LARGE HEATPROOF BOWL** / **SAUCEPAN** / **LOAF TIN** / **BAKING PAPER**

SERVES **12** / PREP **10 MINS** / COOK **5 MINS** + **2 HRS** CHILLING

240g 70% vegan dark chocolate

100g vegan butter or margarine

3 tbsp maple syrup

5 tbsp tahini

150g vegan biscuits, roughly chopped

80g shelled pistachios, roughly chopped

50g dried cranberries

50g Brazil nuts, roughly chopped

1 orange

1 Roughly break up the chocolate with your hands and put it into a large heatproof bowl with the butter and maple syrup. Pour a little water into a pan over a low-medium heat, then place the bowl on top and heat for 5–10 minutes, or until the chocolate mixture has melted.

2 Meanwhile, line the base and sides of a 900g loaf tin with baking paper.

3 Once everything has melted, remove the bowl from the heat and stir in the tahini, biscuits, pistachios, cranberries and Brazil nuts. Then zest the orange and add 1 teaspoon of zest and 1 tablespoon of juice to the bowl. Stir until combined, then transfer the mixture to the lined loaf tin and smooth the top out with a spatula.

4 Transfer the cake to the fridge and leave for at least 2 hours, or until the mixture has set. Store in an airtight container for 6–7 days in the fridge, or freeze for up to a month.

FREEZER-FRIENDLY

GLUTEN-FREE (USE GF BISCUITS)

SPEEDY SALTED CARAMEL CHEESECAKES

These puds have all the flavour and none of the fuss of your typical cheesecake. We use dates to create a gorgeous caramel, which is layered between crushed biscuits and smooth cream cheese. Medjool dates typically have the best caramel flavour, but really any type will do.

EQUIPMENT: SMALL BOWL / MIXING BOWL / WHISK / FOOD PROCESSOR (OPTIONAL)

SERVES 4 / PREP 10 MINS / COOK 0 MINS

8 dates (we use medjool)

6 vegan biscuits
 (we use oat)

150g vegan cream cheese

1 tbsp maple syrup

½ tsp vanilla extract

1 tbsp lemon juice

1 tbsp plant-based milk
 (optional, we use oat)

salt

1 Put the dates into a small bowl and cover with hot water straight from a kettle.

2 Crush the biscuits between your fingers until they are mostly broken down but some big pieces remain. Divide the biscuit pieces among 4 glasses, saving a few to top with later.

3 In a mixing bowl, whisk the cream cheese with the maple syrup, vanilla extract and lemon juice until combined. If the mixture is too thick, add the 1 tablespoon of plant-based milk and continue to whisk until smooth. Taste and add more maple syrup or lemon juice to your liking.

4 Drain the dates, remove the stones and put them into a food processor with 150ml of water and a pinch of salt. Alternatively you can chop the dates finely and combine them with the water and salt in a bowl to create a thick paste.

5 Stir 3 spoonfuls of the blended dates into the cheesecake mixture, then divide among the 4 glasses. Top with the remaining dates, crushed biscuits and a pinch of salt. Serve immediately.

GLUTEN-FREE (USE GF BISCUITS)

LEMON + THYME BISCUITS

You can make these biscuits well ahead of time. First shape the mixture into biscuits and freeze them on a tray. Once solid, put them into an airtight container and separate each biscuit from the next with baking paper. They'll keep for 3 months, and will take 18–20 minutes to bake from frozen.

EQUIPMENT: **MIXING BOWL** / **BAKING PAPER** / **BAKING TRAY**

MAKES **14 BISCUITS** / PREP **10 MINS** + **1 HR** CHILLING / COOK **15 MINS**

120g caster sugar

180g vegan margarine

3 sprigs of fresh thyme, leaves picked

270g plain flour

100g ground almonds

1 lemon

1 Put the sugar and margarine into a mixing bowl and cream together until combined. Add two-thirds of the thyme leaves to the bowl along with the flour, ground almonds, the zest from half the lemon and 1 tablespoon of lemon juice.

2 Mix until combined, then bring the dough together into a ball. Wrap it in baking paper and leave to chill in the fridge for 1 hour.

3 When you're ready to bake the biscuits, preheat the oven to 160°C fan/180°C/gas 4 and line a baking tray with baking paper.

4 Divide the dough into 14 pieces. Roll each piece into a ball, then press into the ball with 3 fingers to flatten it out into a round biscuit shape and create 3 indents along the top. Place each biscuit circle on the lined baking tray and decorate with the remaining thyme leaves.

5 Bake for 15–18 minutes, or until the edges start to brown.

FREEZER-FRIENDLY

ONE-TRAY

MAPLE + GINGER BAKED PLUMS

Locally produced plums come into season during August and September, which is when they're at their juiciest. We love to pair these spiced baked plums with vegan crème fraîche, which you should be able to find at most large supermarkets – but vegan yoghurt is a worthy substitute.

EQUIPMENT: **DEEP BAKING DISH / SMALL BOWL**

SERVES **4** / PREP **3 MINS** / COOK **20 MINS**

4 large ripe plums

½ tsp ground ginger

1 large orange, juice only

3 tbsp maple syrup

2 tbsp almond flakes

8 tbsp vegan crème
   fraîche

1 Preheat the oven to 200°C fan/220°C/gas 7. Slice the plums in half, then remove and discard the stones. Put the plum halves into a deep baking dish and sprinkle them with the ginger. Then drizzle over the juice from the orange, 2 tablespoons of maple syrup and 4 tablespoons of water. Bake for 15–20 minutes, or until softened but holding their shape.

2 Remove the baking dish from the oven, sprinkle the almond flakes over the plum halves and bake for another 5 minutes.

3 Meanwhile, combine the crème fraîche with the remaining 1 tablespoon of maple syrup in a small bowl. Serve the plums alongside the crème fraîche and drizzle over any sticky sauce that's left in the dish.

GLUTEN-FREE
ONE-DISH

CINNAMON SWIRL BANANA BREAD

Cinnamon swirls and banana bread are surely up there among the greatest culinary inventions of all time, so it felt only right to combine two of our favourite things in the world. As always with banana bread, your bananas need to be very ripe so they bring lots of their natural sweetness.

EQUIPMENT: LOAF TIN / BAKING PAPER / MIXING BOWL / SMALL SAUCEPAN / SMALL BOWL

SERVES 10 / PREP 10 MINS / COOK 50 MINS + 5 MINS COOLING

3 ripe bananas
(320g peeled)
75g vegan butter or
margarine, plus extra
250g plain flour
1 tsp baking powder
½ tsp bicarbonate of soda
2 tbsp light brown sugar

FOR THE SWIRL

2 tbsp vegan butter
or margarine
80g dark brown sugar
2 tbsp ground cinnamon
pinch of salt

1 Preheat the oven to 160°C fan/180°C/gas 4. Line the base and sides of a 900g loaf tin with baking paper.

2 Mash the bananas in a mixing bowl until smooth and runny. Melt the 75g of butter either in a microwave or in a small saucepan, then add it to the bowl with the flour, baking powder, bicarbonate of soda and sugar. Stir until well combined.

3 Next, for the swirl, melt the 2 tablespoons of butter in the same pan and combine it in a small bowl with the remaining swirl ingredients (the mixture will be a little on the dry side, but this will create a better swirl).

4 Put a third of the cake mixture into the prepared loaf tin and spread it out evenly. Then add a third of the swirl mixture across the top and run a knife through the cake batter to create a swirl pattern. Repeat twice more, adding more cake mixture then more swirl mixture, and running a knife through it both times. Bake for 50 minutes, or until a skewer inserted comes out clean.

5 Leave the bread to cool slightly for at least 5 minutes before pulling it out of the tin and slicing, then – if you like – serve while warm with a little vegan butter. Stored in an airtight container, this banana bread will keep for 3–4 days at room temperature. Alternatively you can wrap and store it in an airtight container for 1 week in the fridge or 2 months in the freezer.

FRUIT SALAD

WITH ORANGE + CARDAMOM SYRUP

Cardamom really elevates this colourful fruit salad – the chopped seeds bring a warm and piney flavour to the orange syrup. It's a simple addition that adds something extra special to this dessert. We've suggested our favourite fruits, but this is also a great excuse to use up any fruits you already have in the kitchen.

EQUIPMENT: **SMALL SAUCEPAN**

SERVES **4** / PREP **9 MINS** / COOK **3 MINS**

2 cardamom pods,
   seeds finely chopped
   or crushed

1 orange, juice + zest

1 tbsp caster sugar

½ tsp vanilla extract

3 ripe apricots

200g strawberries

100g blueberries

1 Put the crushed cardamom seeds into a small saucepan with the orange juice, caster sugar and vanilla. Boil for 3–4 minutes, or until the mixture thickens into a loose syrup (avoid overcooking the mixture into a thick syrup), then leave to cool.

2 Meanwhile, slice around the stones in the apricots, remove the stones and slice the apricots into wedges. Hull the strawberries and slice them. Put all the fruit on a large serving plate or in a bowl, then pour over the delicious syrup and serve, topped with a pinch of orange zest.

BAKEWELL RICE PUDDING

When cooked, pudding rice has a knack of becoming wonderfully soft and creamy. It's a useful addition, but if need be it can be subbed with basmati or jasmine. This delightful pudding reminds us of our childhoods eating mini bakewell tarts and that irresistible combination of almond and sweet cherries.

EQUIPMENT: **SAUCEPAN / FRYING PAN**

SERVES **4** / PREP **5 MINS** / COOK **35 MINS**

1 tbsp vegan butter
   or margarine

100g pudding rice

500ml almond milk

200ml vegan cream (we
   use oat)

½ tbsp vanilla extract

a handful of flaked
   almonds

1 tbsp maple syrup, plus
   extra

½ tsp almond extract

1 x 400g tin of cherries
   in syrup

1 Melt the butter in a saucepan on a medium heat. Add the rice and toast for 1 minute. Pour in the almond milk, along with the vegan cream and vanilla extract. Bring the pudding to the boil, then reduce the heat and simmer with the lid on for 30–35 minutes, or until the rice is soft and most of the liquid has been absorbed. Meanwhile, heat a frying pan on a medium heat, add the almond flakes and toast for 5 minutes or until golden.

2 Remove the pudding from the heat and stir in the maple syrup and almond extract, then divide among 4 bowls. Drain the cherries, reserving the syrup, and top each bowl with some cherries, some of the reserved cherry syrup and an extra splash of maple syrup. Finish with a sprinkling of toasted almond flakes.

GLUTEN-FREE (USE GF CREAM)

MISO + CARAMEL CHOCOLATE TART

Miso has a habit of making everything taste better. It's the same principle as adding salt – the miso accentuates the chocolate, making it taste richer. Be sure to use 70% dark chocolate because anything higher might not contain the emulsifiers required to prevent the mixture splitting.

EQUIPMENT: SMALL BOWL / FOOD PROCESSOR / 2 MIXING BOWLS / LOOSE-BOTTOMED TART TIN / SAUCEPAN

SERVES **8** / PREP **20 MINS** / COOK **5 MINS** + **2 HRS** CHILLING

12 dates, pitted (we use medjool)

250g vegan biscuits

125g vegan butter or margarine, melted

2 tsp miso paste (we use brown rice miso)

240ml tinned full-fat coconut milk

1 tsp vanilla extract

2 tbsp maple syrup

200g 70% vegan dark chocolate

1 Put the dates into a small bowl and cover with hot water straight from the kettle, then leave to one side. Reserve 1 biscuit to decorate with later, then put the rest of the biscuits into a food processor and pulse until you have fine crumbs. Put the crumbs into a mixing bowl along with the vegan butter or margarine and stir until fully combined.

2 Transfer the biscuit base to a 23cm loose-bottomed tart tin and use your fingers to spread it out evenly across the base and up the sides. Then place the tart in the fridge while you carry out the next steps.

3 Wipe out the food processor. Drain the dates and put them into the processor along with the miso paste, 80ml of coconut milk, the vanilla and 1 tablespoon of maple syrup. Process until smooth, scraping down the sides as you go. Remove the tart from the fridge and, using a spatula, evenly spread the miso caramel filling all across the base. Pop the tart back into the fridge.

4 Pour a couple of centimetres of water into a saucepan over a low heat. Place a metal or glass bowl in the saucepan, making sure the bottom doesn't touch the water. Break the chocolate into the bowl, then add the remaining coconut milk and the rest of the maple syrup. Stir until fully melted, then pour the chocolate into the tin on top of the caramel and tap the tin against the worktop to smooth out the top.

5 Refrigerate the tart for a minimum of 2 hours, or until set. To serve, remove the tart from the tin, finely crush the reserved biscuit and sprinkle it in a circle on top of the tart.

GLUTEN-FREE (USE GF BISCUITS)

NUTRITIONAL INFO

	CALORIES	PROTEIN	FAT	SAT FAT	TOTAL CARBS	SUGAR	FIBRE
AFFOGATO + HAZELNUT BRITTLE	213	1.3g	7.1g	3.4g	35.8g	32.2g	0.5g
AUBERGINE RAGOUT WITH NEW POTATOES (CALCULATED FOR 3 SERVINGS)	466	8.1g	24.2g	3.7g	54.8g	16.6g	11.0g
BAKEWELL RICE PUDDING	379	4.2g	13.7g	1.5g	59.5g	28.9g	2.1g
BANG BANG GREENS	653	20.2g	20.2g	3.1g	96.8g	10.3g	9.3g
BARBECUED MUSHROOM TACOS	880	19.4g	29.5g	8.7g	131.1g	24.4g	9.1g
BEETROOT, CHICORY + WHIPPED FETA SALAD	227	4.4g	21.7g	8.2g	15.9g	10.3g	3.9g
BROTHY KALE + CHICKPEA BOWL	398	16.6g	12.5g	1.5g	55.7g	6.0g	9.7g
BUFFALO CHICKPEA LETTUCE LEAF TACOS	278	9.8g	15.2g	1.5g	23.5g	3.1g	6.6g
BUTTERNUT SQUASH + SAGE GALETTE	564	10.0g	33.2g	13.8g	53.8g	13.1g	4.9g
CABBAGE TAHINI NOODLES (CALCULATED FOR 3 SERVINGS)	450	15.8g	17.6g	2.8g	54.8g	21.7g	14.4g
CAJUN BREADED CAULIFLOWER SALAD (CALCULATED FOR 3 SERVINGS)	448	13.8g	12.0g	1.7g	70.4g	11.4g	7.4g
CAVOLO NERO RISOTTO	434	8.9g	8.1g	2.9g	75.3g	4.2g	4.3g
CELEBRATION CAKE	394	2.2g	16.2g	12.6g	59.4g	45.2g	2.1g
CHARRED CORN SALAD WITH SWEET CHILLI DRESSING	144	3.6g	8.6g	1.2g	13.7g	8.4g	5.3g
CHARRED SPRING ONION + EDAMAME SALAD	456	18.2g	27.7g	3.6g	30.6g	6.6g	9.6g
CHARRED ZA'ATAR CABBAGE WITH LENTIL TABBOULEH	460	20.0g	22.1g	2.0g	38.3g	11.1g	15.3g
CHEAT'S HOT + SOUR SOUP	502	24.8g	10.4g	1.8g	72.4g	7.7g	9.8g

CALORIES	PROTEIN	FAT	SAT FAT	TOTAL CARBS	SUGAR	FIBRE	
490	6.6g	30.5g	13.1g	43.3g	7.0g	3.8g	**CHEESY LEEK + ARTICHOKE CHILLI TART**
469	10.8g	24.4g	10.8g	47.0g	8.8g	5.2g	**CHICKPEA + SPINACH SAMOSA ROLLS**
491	19.1g	9.1g	1.3g	79.3g	6.2g	9.0g	**CHICKPEA 'TUNA' PASTA SALAD** WITH CHARRED SWEETCORN
408	12.9g	15.7g	2.7g	57.6g	16.4g	13.6g	**CHILLI BROCCOLI** WITH SWEET POTATO MASH
429	15.2g	13.5g	9.4g	59.3g	8.2g	13.4g	**CHIPOTLE MOLLETES**
371	5.8g	26.2g	7.3g	27.6g	17.2g	3.6g	**CHOCOLATE ORANGE + TAHINI FRIDGE CAKE**
216	2.4g	8.0g	0.1g	33.7g	14.5g	1.4g	**CINNAMON SWIRL BANANA BREAD**
381	9.8g	12.0g	1.2g	57.2g	6.3g	3.8g	**COCA DE TOMATE**
605	13.6g	27.2g	16.5g	74.9g	15.1g	9.7g	**COCONUT, CHILLI + LIME AUBERGINE CURRY**
625	13.5g	29.9g	3.5g	74.6g	23.5g	6.7g	**CORONATION CAULIFLOWER CIABATTA**
384	9.8g	30.0g	5.6g	18.3g	3.5g	5.5g	**CREAMY AVOCADO SALAD**
515	14.1g	29.7g	3.7g	44.0g	5.2g	8.3g	**CREAMY PASTA E FAGIOLI**
438	8.2g	21.8g	2.8g	50.9g	4.6g	3.9g	**CREAMY PESTO ROSSO GNOCCHI**
439	14.6g	19.3g	2.1g	50.8g	24.0g	9.7g	**CRISPY CABBAGE PANCAKES**
510	32.6g	24.4g	3.9g	39.9g	17.8g	4.5g	**CRISPY CHILLI TOFU SALAD**
366	12.6g	15.3g	2.0g	44.5g	4.5g	5.2g	**CRUNCHY PITTA + HUMMUS NACHOS**
499	16.4g	17.2g	2.7g	74.9g	8.4g	7.4g	**CUMIN ROASTED CAULIFLOWER** WITH COUSCOUS + RED PEPPER SAUCE (CALCULATED FOR 3 SERVINGS)

	CALORIES	PROTEIN	FAT	SAT FAT	TOTAL CARBS	SUGAR	FIBRE
CURRIED TOMATOES + CHICKPEAS ON TOAST	485	19.2g	13.1g	2.0g	73.2g	13.7g	12.1g
DOUBLE BEAN STROGANOFF	517	15.7g	12.0g	1.8g	86.9g	6.4g	11.3g
DOUBLE CHEESE BEETROOT BURGERS	735	22.3g	29.1g	11.8g	93.2g	21.6g	12.1g
FAMILY PASTA TRAYBAKE	513	16.6g	9.2g	3.0g	88.5g	15.1g	6.9g
FIERY PEPPERCORN STIR-FRY	707	30.8g	21.3g	3.4g	102.3g	12.5g	5.0g
FIESTA RICE	479	19.1g	9.9g	1.9g	69.0g	8.4g	23.6g
FRENCH ONION + MUSHROOM STEW WITH GARLIC BREAD	535	15.3g	10.9g	0.6g	89.7g	20.3g	10.1g
FRUIT SALAD WITH ORANGE + CARDAMOM SYRUP	59	1.2g	0.4g	0.0g	13.4g	13.4g	3.4g
GIANT COUSCOUS, LEEK + BROCCOLI	320	5.7g	17.7g	8.0g	26.8g	2.4g	4.0g
GNOCCHI ALL'AMATRICIANA	447	8.3g	14.0g	6.3g	70.4g	7.0g	5.0g
GOOEY CHOCOLATE BROWNIES	409	4.5g	17.6g	5.4g	55.9g	42.3g	4.6g
HARISSA + WALNUT STUFFED COURGETTES	358	7.7g	32.2g	4.2g	8.5g	6.8g	4.3g
HARISSA AUBERGINE ON BUTTER BEAN MASH (CALCULATED FOR 3 SERVINGS)	430	23.0g	12.0g	2.8g	51.5g	12.4g	22.5g
HARISSA BOLOGNESE	488	16.9g	9.2g	2.1g	74.1g	12.3g	10.7g
JAMAICAN TOFU CURRY	501	21.2g	28.3g	4.3g	42.5g	9.8g	8.2g
JEWELLED PERSIAN RICE SALAD	455	8.5g	16.3g	1.9g	69.8g	32.0g	5.6g
KALE + ORANGE SALAD WITH GINGER DRESSING	430	10.0g	25.6g	2.5g	41.0g	39.1g	9.0g

CALORIES	PROTEIN	FAT	SAT FAT	TOTAL CARBS	SUGAR	FIBRE	
178	3.0g	7.9g	1.1g	23.4g	9.0g	1.3g	**LEMON + THYME BISCUITS**
724	9.4g	50.1g	39.9g	59.4g	9.5g	4.3g	**LEMONGRASS + COCONUT CURRY**
783	35.8g	28.1g	4.4g	93.7g	14.3g	9.9g	**LEMON TOFU + NOODLES**
182	2.5g	9.1g	3.1g	23.0g	20.1g	2.7g	**MAPLE + GINGER BAKED PLUMS**
437	16.6g	18.2g	7.3g	46.8g	7.2g	11.0g	**MARMITE PIE**
454	31.3g	22.0g	3.8g	32.4g	7.9g	9.4g	**MASALA TOFU + CARDAMOM RICE**
221	1.6g	9.1g	6.3g	33.5g	29.9g	2.7g	**MERINGUES + CARAMELIZED BANANAS**
237	5.9g	17.3g	3.3g	11.3g	6.5g	5.6g	**MEXICAN LENTIL BOWL** WITH JALAPEÑO DRESSING
554	5.5g	32.9g	12.6g	60.7g	40.4g	6.5g	**MISO + CARAMEL CHOCOLATE TART**
401	15.6g	10.8g	1.3g	58.5g	30.2g	14.2g	**MOROCCAN-STYLE SQUASH + CHICKPEA STEW**
429	10.8g	4.8g	1.0g	82.2g	15.0g	13.6g	**MUSHROOM + DATE PIE**
456	15.7g	15.2g	2.1g	66.0g	9.2g	8.7g	**MUSTARD-CRUSTED CAULIFLOWER STEAKS**
482	26.5g	17.7g	2.7g	49.3g	4.6g	9.2g	**'NDUJA TOFU SCRAMBLE**
618	25.4g	30.0g	4.1g	54.4g	9.6g	16.4g	**NUTTY SUPERFOOD SALAD**
588	18.3g	16.5g	2.1g	89.4g	11.6g	7.6g	**ONE-POT SUN-DRIED TOMATO ORZO**
322	15.5g	6.1g	0.8g	51.0g	21.7g	7.5g	**ONION PAKORAS** WITH LIME SALSA
552	19.4g	20.8g	3.8g	68.6g	13.4g	9.6g	**OUR GO-TO LO MEIN**

	CALORIES	PROTEIN	FAT	SAT FAT	TOTAL CARBS	SUGAR	FIBRE
PEANUT BUTTER AUBERGINE + SMACKED CUCUMBER	347	13.7g	24.7g	4.2g	16.8g	13.6g	9.8g
PEKING 'DUCK' RICE BOWL	408	7.4g	5.6g	0.9g	83.4g	20.7g	6.9g
PERSIAN-STYLE CHICKPEA + WALNUT STEW	637	23.6g	31.6g	4.3g	60.0g	10.2g	13.8g
PORTOBELLO STEAKS + MASH	406	10.8g	17.2g	1.5g	51.1g	6.8g	8.7g
PULLED AUBERGINE BÁNH MÌ	849	24.8g	23.9g	3.0g	142.8g	20.9g	15.2g
RED BEANS + RICE	533	21.8g	6.3g	1.5g	93.3g	6.4g	20.4g
RED PEPPER TAPENADE BAGUETTE PIZZAS	422	13.1g	18.7g	2.0g	50.0g	5.8g	6.5g
RIPE TOMATO + MUSHROOM PASTA (CALCULATED FOR 3 SERVINGS)	487	16.1g	6.9g	1.2g	88.3g	11.0g	6.9g
ROASTED BUTTERNUT SQUASH DHAL WITH CRISPY SHALLOTS	403	25.8g	5.4g	0.8g	66.8g	13.9g	20.5g
ROXY'S BIGOS (CALCULATED FOR 4 SERVINGS)	544	23.5g	9.8g	4.1g	92.0g	14.6g	15.3g
'SALMON' CARROT + MISO BUTTER ON TOAST	529	9.3g	32.0g	3.8g	52.4g	7.1g	8.1g
SAUTÉD COURGETTE WITH TOMATO BULGUR + SUMAC SALT	401	11.4g	10.7g	1.3g	67.6g	5.9g	8.2g
SLOPPY JOE QUESADILLAS	405	11.5g	13.7g	8.6g	58.8g	8.3g	8.4g
SMASHED NEW POTATO SALAD WITH GARLIC DRESSING	344	9.2g	12.3g	1.4g	52.0g	7.9g	7.5g
SPEEDY SALTED CARAMEL CHEESECAKES	244	2.3g	13.1g	9.9g	29.1g	16.2g	2.7g
SPICED APPLE TRAYBAKE PANCAKE	160	2.6g	4.9g	0.2g	26.3g	9.9g	1.5g
SPINACH + ARTICHOKE PASTA	395	13.2g	7.3g	1.5g	68.1g	5.8g	6.0g

CALORIES	PROTEIN	FAT	SAT FAT	TOTAL CARBS	SUGAR	FIBRE	
463	14.5g	22.4g	3.6g	49.0g	10.9g	9.9g	SPINACH + SESAME SALAD
348	12.6g	7.6g	1.2g	59.5g	5.5g	5.3g	SPRING PANZANELLA (CALCULATED FOR 3 SERVINGS)
521	17.2g	18.5g	3.1g	74.5g	17.8g	10.2g	SRIRACHA ROASTED CAULIFLOWER BOWL (CALCULATED FOR 3 SERVINGS)
440	3.2g	23.5g	0.2g	53.8g	26.4g	5.3g	STRAWBERRY DUMP CAKE
241	3.9g	13.1g	5.3g	25.1g	9.1g	2.4g	SUMMER FRUITS + CHIA TART
435	8.1g	13.8g	1.7g	73.8g	25.9g	10.9g	SWEET POTATO + CAULIFLOWER CHAAT (CALCULATED FOR 3 SERVINGS)
740	17.7g	26.4g	16.3g	107.4g	12.0g	11.7g	SWEET POTATO + CHICKPEA TURMERIC CURRY
627	8.9g	21.9g	15.6g	104.9g	18.3g	8.2g	SWEET POTATO KATSU
231	7.0g	13.4g	2.1g	18.5g	5.4g	6.4g	TANGY POPPADOM SALAD
629	26.8g	22.4g	3.2g	74.9g	9.3g	17.1g	TERIYAKI MEATBALL RAMEN
411	20.5g	9.9g	3.9g	56.0g	7.6g	23.9g	THREE BEAN TORTILLA SOUP
629	30.8g	31.9g	3.9g	50.7g	11.3g	10.8g	TOFU LAHMACUN
396	12.9g	7.0g	1.2g	73.1g	26.5g	9.7g	TOMATO + BUTTER BEAN SUMAC SALAD (CALCULATED FOR 3 SERVINGS)
541	13.7g	19.0g	2.8g	83.7g	13.4g	9.5g	TOMATO + FENNEL MACARONI SOUP (CALCULATED FOR 4 SERVINGS)
453	16.0g	19.7g	2.3g	49.6g	8.6g	10.4g	ZA'ATAR VEGGIE FLATBREADS

INDEX

ACKNOWLEDGEMENTS

This book wouldn't have been possible without the hard work and support of so many people.

Thank you to everyone at MJ. A special thanks to our editorial director and commissioning editor, Dan Hurst, for steering the ship. To Aggie Russell, Daniel Prescott-Bennett, Sarah Fraser, Olivia Thomas, Ellie Hughes, Hattie Evans, Ellie Morley and Emma Henderson: thank you for making us feel at home again.

To the dream team: Yuki Sugiura, Frankie Unsworth and Georgia Rudd. Witnessing our food come to life in these gorgeous photographs really was a privilege.

To Zara Murdoch and Anna Dixon: thank you for all your hard work.

To Katy Gilhooly, Annie Lee, Emma Horton, Kay Halsey: thank you for all your work behind the scenes to help us create the best book possible.

To our family and friends. Your continued love and support never goes unnoticed. To Maya and Esi, thank you for everything.

Lastly, a shout out to the amazing SO VEGAN community. Without all of you none of this would be possible.

Big love,

ROXY + BEN, SO VEGAN

PENGUIN MICHAEL JOSEPH

UK | USA | Canada | Ireland | Australia

India | New Zealand | South Africa

Penguin Michael Joseph is part of the Penguin Random House
group of companies whose addresses can be found at
global.penguinrandomhouse.com

First published by Penguin Michael Joseph, 2023

001

Set in Organetto and Gilroy

Colour reproduction by ALTAIMAGE Ltd

Printed and bound in Germany by Mohn Media GmbH

The authorized representative in the EEA is Penguin Random House Ireland,
Morrison Chambers, 32 Nassau Street, Dublin D02 YH68

A CIP catalogue record for this book is available from the British Library

isbn: 978–0–241–61756–4

www.greenpenguin.co.uk

MIX
Paper | Supporting
responsible forestry
FSC® C018179
FSC
www.fsc.org

Penguin Random House is committed to a
sustainable future for our business, our readers
and our planet. This book is made from Forest
Stewardship Council® certified paper.